Introduction

SINCE earliest times, man has fought behind a recognisable sign. Firstly, as a distinguishing mark of his own side, and as a rallying point in the melée of battle. These early symbols were most often a brightly coloured animal or bird.

With the development of body and horse armour in the Middle Ages, this too was covered with colours and devices and brought about the beginning of heraldry.

In the late 16th and early 17th centuries, armies were adopting a more organised arrangement of formations. Pioneered by Gustavus Adolphus, regiments of horse and foot were divided into regular numbers of units, each composed of a definite number of men. This simplification of the way men now fought was reflected, not only in the introduction of the uniform, but also in the symbols that they fought under; the regimental flag had come to stay.

The great respect shown for the Regimental Colours of the modern British army with its sophisticated equipment and tremendous fire power, may seem an anachronism, until one remembers that they represent the real spirit of the regiment. These standards which bear battle honours such as Minden, Waterloo, Alma, Somme, Dunkirk and Korea, are not only a silken history of the regiment, but a focus of pride to those now serving and an object of their loyalty to those, often of the same family, long faded away.

No modeller of military miniatures can doubt the attraction a flag adds to a model. The individual figure is enhanced by its added colour and animation, and is as much a focus of action and interest to the wargamer as the originals were on the battlefield.

The intention of this book is to give both student and modeller a condensed, easy to follow work of reference, using the maximum possible number of illustrations. With this in mind, the coloured drawings are deliberately produced in a flat design format to show the detail and are all to a scale of 54 mm, which matches the 'standard' scale for model soldiers. A number of line drawings and contemporary photographs are also included.

This book covers infantry of the line and the foot guards from the beginnings of the standing army in 1660. The standards and guidons of the cavalry, including their drum banners, will follow in the companion book *British Cavalry Colours.*

The author would like to record his appreciation to Captain A. E. Haswell-Miller for permission to use the cover plate and to *Soldier* magazine for their kind help and loan of photographs.

ABOVE: The Regimental Colours of the 1st Bn, Coldstream Guards 1899 with the RSM in the centre.

FRONT COVER: Ensign and private, 73rd Lord Macleod's Highlanders, 1780. The officer of the 1st Bn, with the Regimental Colour, wears the unusual uniform of the East India Company. The private is shown as he would have fought at the Siege of Gibraltar with the 2nd Bn (Captain A. E. Haswell-Miller).

BACK COVER: Regimental Colour 6th Bn, HLI. It was buff, edged with a mixed red and gold border. The centre containing the regimental title was red with gold borders and lettering, the crown being in full colours with red cap. The wreath was of red roses, pink thistles and green leaves, beneath which was a white scroll with battle honour and a pink thistle with green leaves. The crown and lion on top of staff were gilt, the tassels gold inter-twined with red. Period: 1902-08.

CONTENTS

BRITISH INFANTRY COLOURS

Dino Lemonofides

ALMARK PUBLISHING CO. LTD., LONDON

First Published — February 1971
Reprinted—May 1971
Reprinted—July 1972

ISBN 0 85524 020 2 (hard cover edition)
ISBN 0 85524 021 0 (paper covered edition)

Printed in Great Britain by
Vale Press Ltd., Mitcham, Surrey CR4 4HR
for the publishers, Almark Publishing Co. Ltd.,
270 Burlington Road, New Malden,
Surrey KT3 4NL, England.

Part 1: Colours of the Line Infantry

THE infantry regiments which established the present standing army in 1660 would have fought and been equipped very much as they were in the Civil War. The drawing below shows not only the typical deployment of a regiment at this time but gives a good representation of the design and the number of standards carried.

The colonel's was a plain flag without any design and would correspond to the title of the regiment—ie, the green regiment had green colours. The use of a St George's Cross, depicted in the remaining standards, goes back, at least, to the reign of Richard II and was used by both Royalist and Parliamentary armies. It is still used, as the union flag, on the Queen's Colour of the Guards regiments and was a feature of infantry

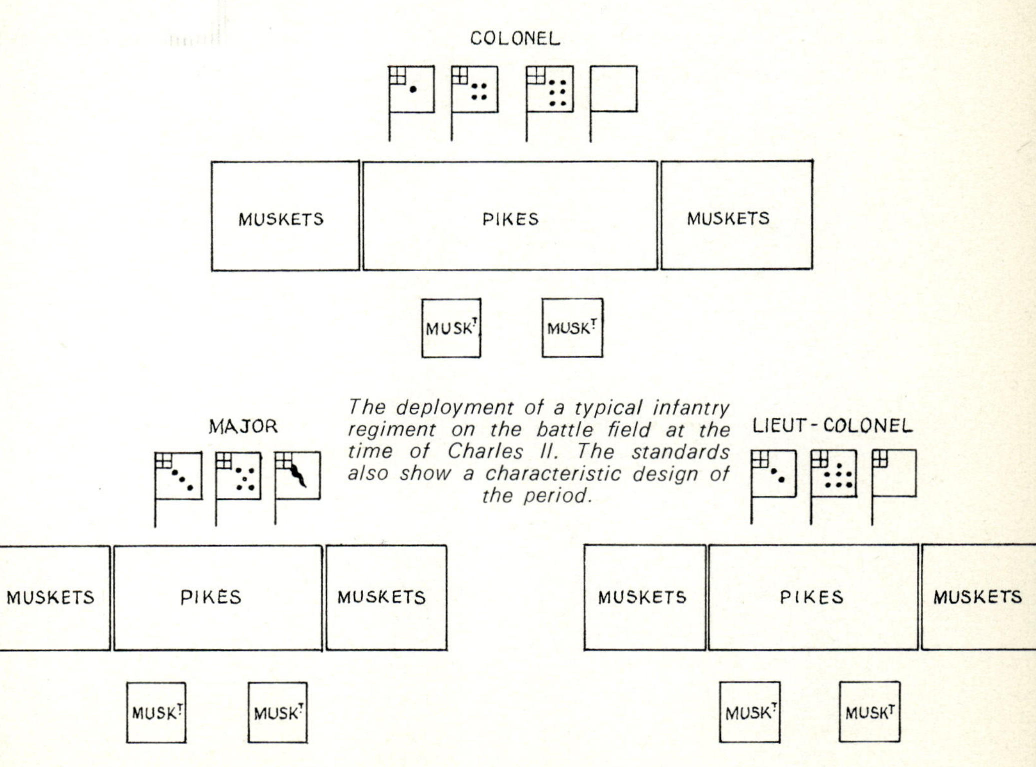

The deployment of a typical infantry regiment on the battle field at the time of Charles II. The standards also show a characteristic design of the period.

colours until 1881. The curious tail like symbol on the Major's standard is now known as a 'pile wavy' and again survives on some Guards colours. Each captain in descending seniority added another symbol, a star, ball, lozenge, etc, to his ensign; first captain—one ball; second captain—two balls, and so on.

After the Restoration, Charles II quickly established bodies of personal troops, or foot guards, which are now the three senior regiments in the Brigade of Guards (now called the Guards Division). These regiments, because of their close association with the Sovereign, have always followed a different set of regulations regarding their colours. For ease of reference these are dealt with later in this book.

1660-1747

This span of 87 years saw not only domestic strife in England, Ireland and Scotland, but the Marlborough Wars and conflicts with Holland, Spain, France and in North America. It is not surprising that it also saw the rapid growth of the British navy and army.

Royal Warrants were given to noblemen, loyal to the sovereign, to raise and maintain regiments. Their influence was such that they almost owned the regiment and, to a large degree, used their own discretion regarding uniforms and equipment. This was emphasised, particularly on the colours, by adding some personal emblem as a distinguishing mark.

In 1707 the infantry was reorganised and the number of ensigns reduced to three. Also in this year, the small St George's Cross, which had already grown to cover the entire flag, was joined by the white saltire and blue field of St Andrew, to mark the political union of England and Scotland.

THE REGULATIONS OF 1747, 1751 AND 1768

The details given in the Clothing Regulations of 1747 and the Royal Warrants of 1751 and 1768 now officially established the principles of size, colour and design of infantry colours. Subsequent regulations, given through the years, have only introduced modifications on points of detail.

The main features of the 1747 regulations were:

(1) To forbid Colonels to 'put his Arms, Crest, Device or Livery on any part of the Appointments of the Regiment under his command'; this included Colours, drummers coats and drums, grenadier caps and Bells of Arms.

(2) To reduce the number of Colours to two per battalion. These to be a King's or First Colour—The Great Union—and 'the Second Colour to be the Colour of the Facing of the Regiment with the Union in the upper canton, except those Regiments which are faced with White or Red, whose Second Colour is to be the Red Cross of St George on a white ground and the Union in the upper canton'.

(3) This also went on to give details of the central design which was to be painted or embroidered in gold Roman characters the number of the rank of regiment within a wreath of roses and thistles on the same stalk. The rank of the regiment meant the order the regiment stood in the precedence table.

(4) A list was included of those regiments granted special badges and states that the number of the rank of the regiment was to be towards the upper corner. The list and special badges are given opposite.

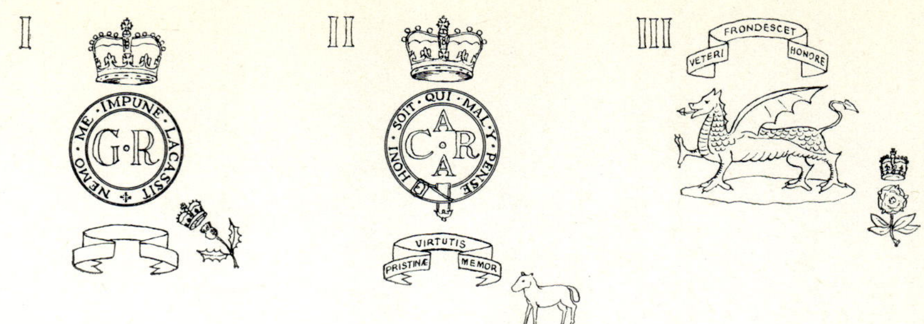

1st or Royal Regiment (Royal Scots)

Blue, with 'GR' in gold on a blue field within the green circle of St Andrew. In the three corners a crown and thistle; scroll without motto.

2nd or Queens Own Royal Regiment (Royal West Surrey Regiment)

Sea green, with 'CARA' in gold on red within the garter (garter blue), in the three corners the white lamb; scroll with motto 'PRISTINAE VIRTUTIS MEMOR.'

NB: The letters 'CR' stand for Carolina Regina and the two A's the terminal letters of the previous words.

3rd or the Buffs (East Kent Regiment)

Buff, with a green dragon above the scroll with 'VETERI FRONDESCET HONORE'. In the three corners a crown and rose (crimson).

NB: No crown above badge.

4th or Kings Own Royal Regiment (Royal Lancaster Regiment)

Blue, 'GR' in gold on a red field within the garter and plain white scroll below. In the three corners the crowned lion of England in gold.

NB: No scroll on King's colours.

5th Regiment (The Northumberland Fusiliers)

Pale yellow, St George in white armour on a brown horse, and green dragon. In the three corners a crown and rose.

NB: No crown above badge.

6th Regiment (The Royal Warwickshire Regiment)

Deep yellow, in the centre a white antelope on a green mount; plain scroll. In the three corners a crown and rose.

NB: No crown above badge.

7th or the Royal English Fusiliers (The Royal Fusiliers)
Blue, a red rose in a red field within the garter; plain scroll. In the three corners the white horse on a green mount.

8th or The King's Regiment (Liverpool Regiment)
Blue, the white horse on a red field within the garter; scroll with motto 'NEG ASPERA TERRENT'. In the three corners 'GR' and crown in gold.

18th The Royal Irish (The Royal Irish Regiment)
Blue, a gold harp; motto 'VIRTUTIS NAMURCENSIS PRAEMIUM'. In the three corners the golden lion of Nassau in a blue field, surrounded by golden billets.

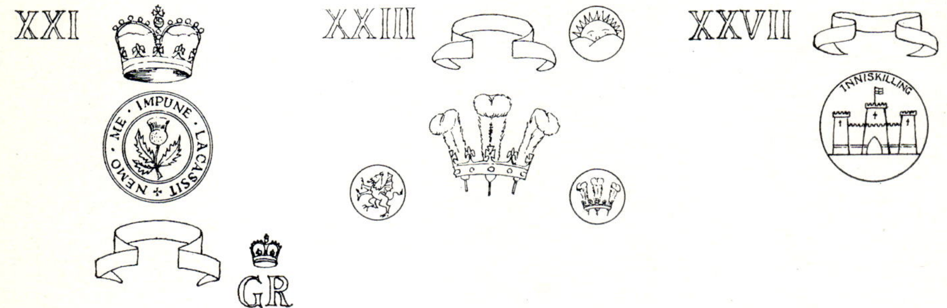

21st or Royal North British Fusiliers (The Royal Scots Fusiliers)
Blue, the thistle on a blue ground within the green circle of St Andrew. In the three corners 'GR' and crown in gold. Plain scroll.

23rd or The Royal Welch Fusiliers (The Royal Welch Fusiliers)
Blue, three white feathers issuing for a golden Prince's coronet. Scroll with motto 'ICH DIEN'. In the upper corner a gold sun rising behind a green hill, blue sky. A red dragon on blue field, lower left hand corner and the three feathers and coronet on a red field in the lower right hand corner.

NB: No crown above badge and no label on the King's colour.

27th or The Inniskilling Regiment (The Royal Inniskilling Fusiliers)
Buff, the castle of Inniskilling white in a blue field and 'INNISKILLING' in gold; plain scroll.

NB: No crown above badge.

The list in the Royal Clothing Warrant of 1747 is repeated in Appendix 1 page 46.

This is the first time reference is made of special badges for line regiments but it would seem this was confirming something already in practice. Although no reason is given, most of these corps are, in fact, Royal regiments, so the association is obvious.

Mention is also made of Marine Regiments; six were raised in 1739 and numbered 44th to 49th of the Line. Both their Colours were to show

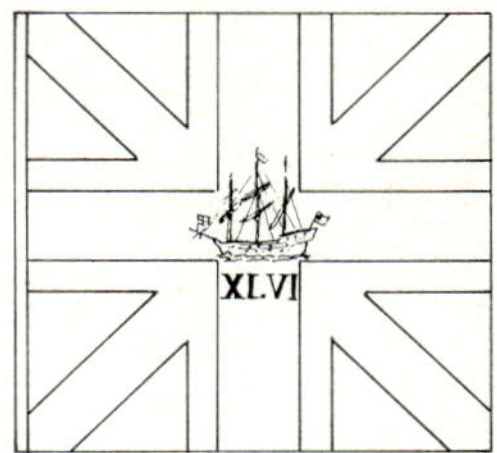

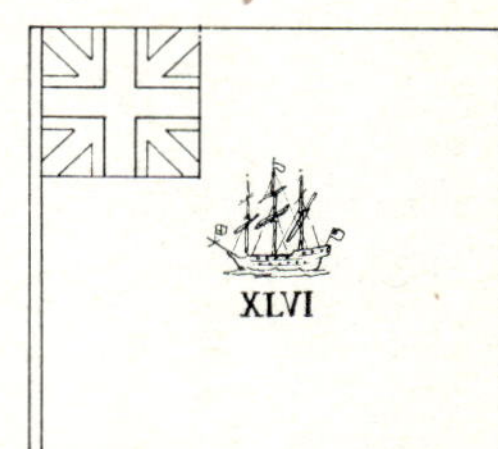

A pair of Colours for the 46th Marine Regiment raised in 1739. The regimental colour for all six regiments, 44th to 49th, was yellow and of the same basic design. These troops were part of the Infantry of the Line, until disbanded in 1748.

a 'Ship with Sails furled and the rank of the regiment underneath'; all second Colours were yellow.

It is obvious, from the similarity of the wording, that the 1747 Clothing Regulations were the basis of the Royal Warrant of 1751. Most of the new regulations affected the cavalry and the only important item regarding infantry colours was that the addition of the 'pile wavy' descending from the upper corner of each colour was to be used to distinguish the second battalion's Colours.

The Royal Warrant of 1768 is again very similar to those of 1743 and 1751 and varies only on two important points.

(1) Exact measurements of Colours and pike are given for the first time.

(2) Those regiments with black facings receive mention and their Second Colour was required 'to be St George's Cross throughout; Union in the Upper Canton; the other three Black'.

The regiments which wore black facings in 1768 were the 50th—later 1st Battalion The Queen's Own Royal West Kent Regiment; 58th—later 2nd Battalion The Northamptonshire Regiment; the 64th—later the North Staffordshire Regiment and the 70th—later the 2nd Battalion The East Surrey Regiment.

Although the early warrants stated that the colours of the marching regiments were to be of the same size as the Foot Guards these were called for 'as of the usual largeness'. At the coronation of James II the colours of the Guards were 8ft 3in flying by 7ft 6in on the staff. By 1747 these had been reduced to 6ft 6in by 6ft 2in but no precise dimensions are laid down until the warrant of 1768 when they were regulated at 6ft 6in horizontal by 6ft vertical, and the staff at 6ft 10in overall.

1768-1881

No fundamental changes were made to infantry ensigns during this time. However, there were modifications, trends in interpretation of design and changes in designation. A summary of the main points is given, broadly in chronological order.

1768: Although the details of the central decoration were given in the regulations of 1747, its interpretation was left to the regiment, or rather the colonel commanding, whose duty to provide colours was ordered until 1857. It is difficult, therefore, to be specific regarding its design from regiment to regiment, or year to year, particularly as Colours were held for a number of years.

The small neat design of 1751 gave way, from about 1760, to a flamboyant and rambling arrangement with the rank number in a red cartouche of rococo design. The rose changed from the heraldic Tudor

The three drawings show the typical interpretation in the design of the union wreath between 1750 and 1780. Left is the neat design of 1751 which gave way to the flamboyant rococo design in 1760 (centre). Right is the return to a more symmetrical shape in 1780, which lasted for many years.

type to look more like the ordinary garden variety. Other regiments dispensed with the wreath altogether, replacing it with the formal design of the garter.

By the 1780s the wreath had reverted to its former symmetrical shape, but larger than before, and a red shield with formal edging now held the number.

1784: Four regiments, 12th (Suffolk), 39th (Dorsetshire), 56th (2nd Essex) and the 58th (2nd Northamptonshire) were granted the honour title 'GIBRALTAR' for their services during the siege of the rock from 1779 to 1783.

The first infantry regiment to receive a distinction for service in battle was the 18th Foot (The Royal Irish) who were awarded a badge, the Lion of Nassau and the motto 'VIRTUTIS NAMURCENSIS PROEMIUM'

The Regimental Colour of the 39th Foot (Dorsetshire Regt) in 1785. The battle honour 'GIBRALTAR' was granted in 1784, one of the first ever. Three other regiments also hold this honour, the 12th (Suffolk), 56th (2/Essex) and the 58th (2/Northamptonshire Regt).

A Regimental Colour of the 78th Highland Regiment, 1790. It was buff in colour, 6ft 6in by 6ft and carried on a pike staff 9ft 10in long.

by William III for valour at Namur in 1695. These were included as part of the special badges given in the Clothing Regulation of 1747.

The 'Gibraltar Regiments', however, seem to have set the pattern for what is now common practice. Incidentallly, the Colours of the 12th, said to have been with the regiment during the siege, bear the motto 'STABILIS', the only known example of a Line Regiment bearing a motto not granted by Royal Warrant.

It is appropriate to mention here that these four regiments were later authorised, between 1827 and 1836, to bear the badge Castle and Key superscribed 'GIBRALTAR' and the motto 'MONTIS INSIGNIA CALPE' on their Colours. In 1907 this grant was also extended to the Highland Light Infantry, who as the original 73rd fought at the siege; dates were added in 1909 to distinguish this from another Gibraltar honour.

1801: With the Union of Great Britain and Ireland the red saltire of St Patrick completed the union flag that we know today. The shamrock was also included in the wreath which was to become known as the union wreath. In all probability these details were added to existing colours.

In this year the battle honour 'MINDEN', fought on August 1, 1759, was awarded to the 12th Foot (The Suffolk Regiment), 20th (The Lancashire Fusiliers), 23rd (The Royal Welch Fusiliers), 25th (The King's Own Scottish Borderers), 37th (The Royal Hampshire Regiment) and the 51st (King's Own Yorkshire Light Infantry).

The shield for the central ornament began to be changed to a circular crimson patch bearing the regiment's numeral and surrounded by its title. Since 1782 the majority of regiments had as their secondary title a county title.

1802: A Horse Guards Letter dated July 6th awarded over forty regiments the battle honour 'EGYPT' to mark the successful campaign against the French in 1801. This took the form of a badge, the Sphinx, superscribed 'EGYPT' and is usually shown with a small wreath of immortelles underneath.

It is now the most common honour badge to be found on today's Colours.

Honours for the Battle of Maida (July 4, 1806) were granted in 1807 and some honours for the Peninsular War (1808-1814) were awarded during the campaign. It was now clear that the custom was well established and since this time all campaigns of importance have been commemorated.

1818-1830: This was a period of great activity and interest in the design of richly decorated and elegant uniforms, certainly in many ways a reaction from the hard campaigning of the Napoleonic Wars.

Many regiments had new pairs of Colours presented at this time, the old ones probably mere shreds after the rigours of the Peninsula. A general trend to a more overall symmetry seemed to be the vogue, the

The Regimental Colour of the 31st Foot c. 1850. Battle honours authorised in 1847 are shown on this colour; the ground was buff coloured, the facing colour of the 31st before becoming the 1st Battalion East Surrey Regiment in 1881 when the facings were changed to white. The Colour shown above it is the Queen's Colour, which was based on the Union Flag with the regimental number and Royal crown in gold lace. It is of interest that though the regulations of 1844 called for the the First Colour to be called 'Royal' this contemporary print still calls it the 'Queen's'.

Imperial Crown became a usual feature and battle honours, by now more often a single name, were inscribed on a small scroll.

1844: This year saw the first regulations in Queen Victoria's long reign; as far as Infantry Colours are concerned, the main changes were:

(1) The First or King's Colour was now to be called 'The Royal', a term which lasted until 1892 when it was altered to 'The Queen's'.

(2) The second Colour was now officially called 'Regimental'.

(3) The central design was laid down. 'Regiments which bear a Royal, County, or other Title are to have such designation on a red ground, a circle within the Union Wreath of Roses, Thistles and Shamrocks. The number of the Regiment in Gold Roman characters in the centre'.

(4) All devices, distinctions and battle honours had been, up until this time, placed on both Colours; under these regulations they were to be shown on the Regimental or second Colour only.

1855: The size of Colours was ordered to be 6ft horizontal by 5ft 6in vertical in this year.

1858: The size of Colours was now ordered to be 4ft horizontal by 3ft 6in vertical, and the spear point on the colour pike was replaced with the Royal Crest similar to the existing pattern. In a Horse Guard's letter of July 5, 1859, the fringes which had always been part of Cavalry Colours were added to those of infantry. Apparently, because of their reduced size they had 'a poor effect on Parade'. The instructions also required the border fringes for the Queen's Colour to be crimson silk and gold and the Regimental Colour, of the facings of the corps to be gold.

The central design had almost reached its final form. The red circular ground was of uniform size and the Union Wreath of even symmetry with the arrangement of the roses, thistles and shamrocks of the set pattern still used today. Battle honour scrolls were generally placed in two vertical rows either side of the central motif and battle honour badges near the lower edge with the Sphinx always in the centre. Those regiments who were allowed to display special badges showed the central one within the Union Wreath and the smaller ones in each corner except the upper canton which, of course, still held the Union flag.

1868: This year's Queen's Regulations ordered another reduction in the size of Colours to 3ft 9in horizontal by 3ft vertical, exclusive of a 2in fringe. This size has remained unchanged up to the present time.

By this time, because of the change in tactics on the battlefield, the Colours were now serving a purely symbolic and ceremonial function. The last recorded action when they were carried is at Laings Nek in South Africa (January 28, 1881) by the 58th (2nd Battalion Northamptonshire Regiment) and these colours, presented in 1860, were still used by the regiment when it amalgamated with The Royal Lincolnshire Regiment (10th Foot) to form the 2nd East Anglian Regiment in 1960.

1873: The Colour pike, 9ft 10in long since 1768, was regulated to 8ft 7in long. Under this set of Queen's Regulations 'II BATT.' was to be placed on a scroll below the Union Wreath in the case of 2nd Battalions.

ABOVE LEFT: Royal Scots (1st Foot) Regimental Colour of 1751. Colour was dark blue with the Union in the top left hand corner. The centre circle green with motto and borders yellow. Within the circle on a dark blue ground was the Royal Cypher in gold. Beneath this is a plain white scroll. The crowns and thistles are in 'proper' colours. The flaming ray of gold (pile wavy) was the distinction of the 2nd Battalion. RIGHT: Black Watch Regimental Colour of the 1840s. Colour was dark blue with the Union top left, a blue garter with gold border and lettering, the centre red with gold cypher and numeral, and crown in full colours with roses red, thistles pink, leaves green. Scrolls were gold, the Sphinx was silver, and tassel and pike head gold.

Part 2: Regimental Colours of Infantry of the Line, 1881

GENERAL Orders 41 and 70 saw a major reorganisation of Infantry of the Line and to appreciate its effect on their Colours one must look closer at what was to become known as the 'Cardwell System'.

Basically, the British Isles was divided into 70 Regimental Districts, each one allotted an Infantry Regiment of two Regular (or Line) Battalions and two Militia Battalions of what was termed a Territorial Regiment. The main point of the system was one regular battalion of each regiment was to be stationed at home and provide reinforcements for the other serving overseas. The home battalion recruited from its district, so as to ensure one battalion was always up to strength, and was supported by its Militia Battalions in the case of war.

All single battalion regiments (except the Cameron Highlanders) were amalgamated in pairs, each pair forming one regiment.

All infantry regiments ceased being designated by the number allotted in 1747 and were reallocated, and known, by a territorial or other descriptive title.

The rationalisation to a basic pattern of uniform also called for facings to be Blue for Royal Regiments, White for English and Welsh, Yellow for Scottish and Green for Irish Regiments.

Rifle Regiments were to wear green uniforms with regimental facings and not carry colours.

The main effect on regimental colours are listed below:

(a) The Royal or First Colour remained the Great Union.

(b) The Regimental or Second Colour was to be the colour of the facing of the Regiment, except those regiments with white facings in which case this was to be the Red Cross of St George in a white field. In effect this applied to all English and Welsh Regiments whose facings were now white. The small union in the upper canton disappeared.

(c) The territorial designation, with its Royal or other title, was to be

---

OPPOSITE PAGE: These are the colours of the 2nd Battalion of the King's Own, The Royal Lancaster Regiment. They were presented by Queen Victoria at Windsor Castle on December 6, 1878, when the Battalion was on eve of embarking for the Zulu war. They are the fringed 4ft by 3ft 6in pattern and were laid-up in 1926.

CORUNNA
SALAMANCA
PENINSULA
WATERLOO
INKERMAN
ABYSSINIA

The Queen's and Regimental Colours of the 1st Bn Royal Sussex Regiment posed by the colour party and escort in 1899, prior to a laying-up ceremony after presentation of new colours.

shown within a crimson circle, surmounted by the Imperial Crown on both Colours, but on the Regimental or Second Colour only, it was to be surrounded by the Union Wreath.

(d) The Colours of the 1st and 2nd Battalions were to bear the ancient badges, devices, distinctions and mottos conferred by Royal authority. The 3rd and 4th Battalions were to carry the same Colours without the distinctions, devices, etc. In practice these badges were shown in the centre of the crimson circle, the smaller distinctions in each of the four corners.

The number of the battalion, I, II, III or IV to be placed in the upper canton.

1

2

3

4

5

6

Plate 1

(1) Regimental Colour, 3rd Foot or The Buffs, 1751. This Colour shows the special badges granted in the 'Cloathing Warrant' of 1747. (2) Regimental Colour, 12th Foot, The East Suffolk Regiment, 1781. (3) First or King's Colour, 21st Foot, Royal North British Fuzileers, 1807. (4) Regimental Colour, 5th or Northumberland Regiment of Foot, 1807. (5 and 6) These show the central design of the King's and Regimental Colours of the 12th Foot, The East Suffolk Regiment, 1807.

The Queen's (left) and Regimental colours of the Black Watch in 1895 with escort of colour sergeants. The Regimental colour has the laurel wreath design with scrolls entwined bearing the battle honours.

(e) A modification to this rule was made in 1885 which stated that those regiments not entitled to a Royal or ancient badge, the number of the Battalion will be placed within the crimson circle bearing the name of the regiment instead of in the upper or dexter canton.

In 1894 this was again modified 'in the case of regiments which are entitled to carry honorary distinctions in all four corners of the Colours, the number of the battalion is to be placed below the honorary distinction' in the dexter canton.

One of the outcomes of this enormous reorganisation, not readily accepted by many regiments, was that the amalgamation of two corps necessitated in the bringing up to date of the Colours. All battle honours, distinctions, etc, of the individual regiments under the old regime were now shared by both battalions of the new regiment.

Some were issued with new colours, others grimly held on and modified their pre-1881 Colours which served for many years, proudly maintaining a link with the past.

Although not specified in the 1881 Regulations, a circular laurel wreath was incorporated to bear the battle honour scrolls. This design feature was officially approved in 1909, which required '. . . Regiments where the number of actions exceeds nine, laurel branches are to be introduced and scrolls bearing the names of the Actions entwined thereon'.

Many regiments were never issued with the Colours laid down by 1881 Regulations for almost immediately they were changing back to the old facing colours. The Buffs (Royal Kent Regiment), naturally, were

Queen Victoria inspects the colour party of the 1st Bn, The Gordon Highlanders, on September 18, 1899, just after they had been presented with new colours at Ballater by the Prince of Wales, their Colonel-in-Chief. Shortly after this the battalion left for active service against the Boers in South Africa.

one of the first to change back. They were issued with a stand of Colours in 1864, the second or Regimental, being buff. Although under the Cardwell reform this was now to be the St George's Cross on White (white facing), when they were next presented a pair of Colours, in 1892, the Regiment's facings were now ordered back to being buff. In fact, the Second Battalion were issued with the St George's cross on white Regimental Colours in 1886, but this was replaced by a buff Colour without ceremony in 1891.

The addition of the laurel branches formed around the union wreath was the final feature which brings the design up to date. Apart from the changing back to the old facing colours for many regiments, in 1930 the King approved of all infantry regiments having a central badge.

The only other major change affected the First, or King's Colour, The Great Union. Because of the shortage of space on some regiments' Regimental Colours, battle honours for The Great War, 1914-1919, and later for the Second World War, 1939-1945, were placed on the horizontal limb of the St George's Cross of the Union. It was also found necessary to restrict these to ten selected honours for each war.

The 1957 White Paper which has had as profound an effect on the reorganisation of the army as the 'Cardwell System' had in 1881 has, in fact, changed the actual design of Regimental Colours hardly at all. As the regiments have amalgamated, the badges have been redesigned to incorporate the distinctive features of both the old regiments. The number of battle honour scrolls on both the Queen's and Regimental Colours have been increased again to include all the actions of combined corps. This has been done with a high degree of taste and skill and today's Colours are indeed a thing of beauty in their own right.

THE ROYAL MARINES

The six marine regiments, given precedence of 44th to 49th in the Line and whose Colours are mentioned in the Clothing Warrant of 1747,

Officers and NCOs of 2nd Bn Seaforth Highlanders pictured at Ferozepore with the honorary Assaye Colour. This is the 1899 replica of the 1803 original. It is in buff silk with the Elephant device and 'LXXVIII' within a laurel wreath. 'Assaye' is on a scroll above.

were disbanded in 1748. When raised again in 1755 they were placed under Admiralty control and have been ever since.

One custom they maintain from the days when they were regiments of the Line is the right to carry Colours and although it is beyond the scope of this book to cover the history of their development, one or two interesting features of their present design are included for interest.

The coloured illustration of the present Colours shows the blue second colour of a 'Royal' regiment granted to the corps by George II in 1802. The single battle honour 'GIBRALTAR' in, in fact, for the capture of the Rock in 1704 and not in its defence; however, the laurel wreath is also in honour of capturing an island, that of Belle Isle, off the coast of Brittany, in 1761. In 1827 George IV directed that the laurel wreath encircling the globe should be in the corps distinguishing badge and added a special distinction, that of his own Cypher, which was to appear for ever on the Colours.

HONORARY COLOURS

Three line regiments, the 74th—later 2nd Battalion The Highland Light Infantry, 76th—later 2nd Battalion The Duke of Wellington's Regiment, and the 78th—later 2nd Battalion The Seaforth Highlanders, have the special distinction of carrying Honorary Colours granted by The Honorable East India Company. In the case of the 74th and 78th Regiments this was for distinguished service at the Battle of Assaye on September 23, 1803, colours being presented the same year.

7

8

9

10

11

12

Plate 2

(7) Regimental Colour, 4th Foot, King's Own Regiment, 1808. (8) Second or Regimental Colour, 9th Foot, East Norfolk Regimental, 1807. (9) Regimental Colour, 12th Foot, East Suffolk Regiment, 1849; presented in 1849 and laid-up in 1955. (10) Regimental Colour, 7th Foot or The Royal Fuzileers, 1808. (11) Regimental Colour, 1st Battalion, The Royal Lincolnshire Regiment. Presented in 1864 and carried until amalgamation in 1960. (12) Regimental Colour, 1st Battalion, Wiltshire Regiment. This Colour was used from 1865 until 1939.

The original 'Assaye Colour' of the 74th was lost in a fire in Ireland in 1918, its remains are a treasured possession of the regiment. Subsequent replica Colours were given to the regiment, one privately, and when this was laid up in 1931, a replacement was presented by the City of Glasgow. This Colour is still carried by the 1st Battalion The Royal Highland Fusiliers. It is white, 3ft 9in by 3ft and fringed. In the centre, within a green laurel wreath, an elephant above the Roman numerals LXXIV. Above, a blue scroll, edged yellow 'ASSAYE' and in the base a blue scroll edged yellow 'SERINGAPATAM'.

The fate of a similar colour presented to the 78th remains unknown. One or two attempts to authorise its replacement were turned down by the Horse Guards although it had no objection to a third colour being displayed in the Officer's mess, provided it was not carried on parade. A replica colour was purchased in 1889 and is buff bearing the elephant and LXXVIII within a laurel wreath and above on a blue scroll 'ASSAYE'.

The old 76th—now The Duke of Wellington's Regiment—not only still carry a pair of Honorary Colours, granted for distinguished service, but the original spearheads on the Colour pikes, specially engraved by the Honorable East India Company are transferred to each new stand of colours. These are of the old 6ft 6in by 6ft size, one being the Great Union and the second, the Red Cross of St George on a white field, with a small Union in the dexter canton. The devices and battle honours appear on both colours, as does the number of the regiment, LXXVI, in the upper canton. The design shows the Elephant with Howdah and Mahout in the centre circumscribed 'HINDOOSTAN', surrounded by a Union Wreath and the Imperial Crown above. The battle honours are 'ALLY GHUR', 4th SEPTEMBER, 1803; 'DELHI', 11th SEPTEMBER, 1803; 'AGRA', 10th OCTOBER, 1803; 'LESWAREE', 1st NOVEMBER, 1803; 'DEIG', 23rd DECEMBER, 1804; 'MYSORE', 'NIVE'; 'CORUNNA' and 'PENINSULA'.

The original pair of Colours were presented in 1808 and used until 1830, the second was in use 1830-1888, the third pair 1888-1901. This pair was lost in the fire at Rangoon in 1901. A fourth pair was presented together with a pair of the regulation pattern in 1906 and replaced by a new stand in 1969.

Two other regiments own third colours, the 2nd Foot—later the Queen's Royal Regiment (West Surrey) and the 5th Foot—later The Royal Northumberland Fusiliers. Both these colours are honorary but are never allowed to be carried in the ranks.

The Royal Northumberland Fusiliers always observed St George's Day, when the green 'Drummer's Colour', as it is called, is officially allowed to appear. The new regiment, 1st Battalion, The Royal Regiment of Fusiliers still retains this colour and ceremony.

OPPOSITE PAGE: The photograph, taken at Pietermaritzburg, Natal, 1899 is of the Regimental Colours of the 2nd Battalion Duke of Wellington's Regiment. The large standards in front are the Honorary colours given by the East India Company in 1829. Note the spearheads on the pikes of the honorary colours, as described above in the text.

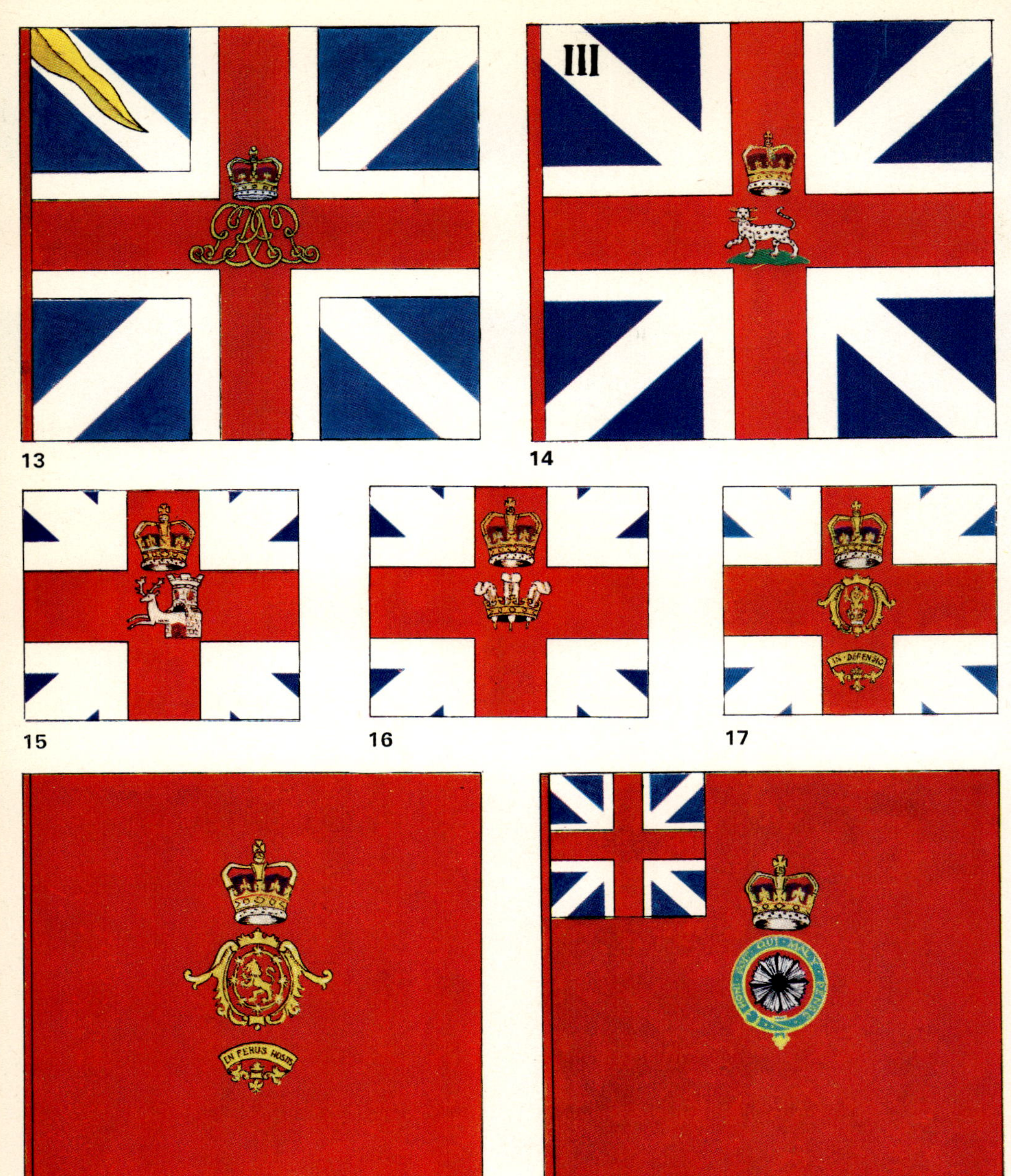

Plate 3: Guards Brigade

(13) Major's Colour, 1st Foot Guards (Grenadier), 1750. This later became the King's Colour of the 3rd Battalion. (14) Regimental Colour, 2nd Foot Guards (Coldstream) with the badge of the 3rd Company, 1750. (15, 16, 17) Central detail of Regimental Colours for: (15) 23rd Company, 1st Foot Guards, 1750. (16) 3rd Company, 2nd Foot Guards, 1750. (17) 1st Captain's Company, 3rd Foot Guards, 1750. (18) Colonel's Colour, 3rd Foot Guards (Scots), 1751. (19) Lieut-Colonel's Colour, 2nd Foot Guards (Coldstream), 1751.

20

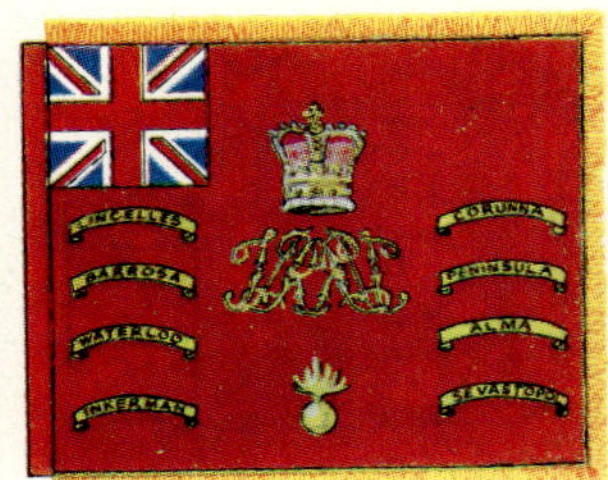

21

22

23

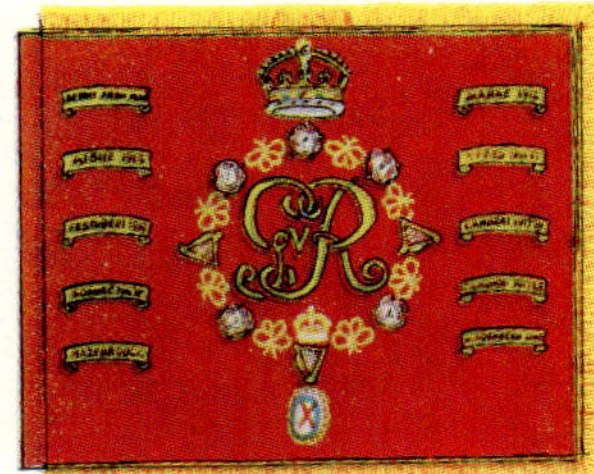

24

25

26

27

Plate 4: Guards Brigade

(20) The State Colour, Scots Guards. Presented by Queen Victoria in 1899 and still carried by Guards of Honour mounted on state occasions at which the Sovereign is present. (21) Queen's or Lieut-Colonels Colour, 2nd Battalion, Grenadier Guards, 1896. (22) Regimental Colour, 1st Battalion, Scots Guards, 1896. Showing the central badge of the 9th Company. (23) Kings or Major's Colour, 3rd Bn Coldstream Guards, 1932. This colour shows the 'pile wavy', the distinguishing mark of a Major's standard as far back as 1642. (24) King's Colour, 1st Battalion, Irish Guards, 1927. (25) King's Colour, 1st Battalion, Welsh Guards, 1927. (26) Regimental Colour, 1st Bn Coldstream Guards, with the badge of the 22nd Company. (27) Regimental Colour, 1st Bn Irish Guards, with the badge of the 3rd Company.

Part 3: Colours of the Foot Guards

TRADITION has perhaps a stronger hold in the Guards than in any other regiment and is nowhere better shown than in their Regimental Colours. Throughout three hundred years of history, authority has many times tried to make them conform to a more general set of regulations as laid down for line regiments. It is no surprise, least of all to the Guards and like in so many other disputes, that they won the day eventually.

Although the actual size of the Colours has generally been the same as those of Line Infantry, in most other respects they follow a separate set of rules and it would be as well to establish, at the beginning what these main differences are.

(1) As well as a pair of Regimental Colours, the three senior regiments, Grenadier, Coldstream and Scots Guards now carry, in addition, a Royal Standard or State Colour.

(2) The Queen's or First Colour is crimson and Regimental or Second Colour is the Great Union.

(3) All battle honours are placed on both Queen's and Regimental Colours.

(4) Each company of all five Guards regiments have their own Company Badge which is borne in rotation in the centre of the Regimental Colour. These badges are also shown on a small Company Colour.

The regulations and basic design adopted at the formation of the three senior regiments, that is between 1660 and 1661 are broadly the same today. Another look at the line drawing, Fig 1, may help to explain this.

The three senior officers standards were of simple design, with the addition of the crown and royal cypher to mark them as household troops. The multiple symbols design which distinguished the first, second and third Captains' flag were gradually, between 1660 and 1712, replaced by royal or other badges, usually heraldic in origin, each Captain's company having his own badge.

When Company Colours were abolished for the infantry they continued to be issued to the Guards until 1838, when only one Regimental Colour was provided for each battalion. The system of a different company badge being selected to be placed on each new issue of Colours dates from that year. Although all companies were issued with Colours until 1838 only two were actually carried.

Regulations in 1855 abolished the system whereby Colonels provided the regiment's Colours. The state now undertook to do this and not only restated that this was to be the Great Union, 1st Colour, appropriate

Part of the Colour Guard, Grenadier Guards, in 1896. Queen's or First Colour is on the left and the Regimental or Second Colour is on the right. Design details are described in the text and drawn in colour on page 25. Note the position of the Lee-Metford at the 'shoulder', carried in a similar fashion to the earlier muskets.

The colours of the 1st Battalion, Grenadier Guards, 1896. The Regimental Colour (right) bore the badge of the 20th Company at this time. Shown in the picture (left to right) are a corporal drummer, drum-major, drummer, the adjutant and the Lieut-Col commanding the battalion.

hue as for the Regimental Colour, but intended this to include all foot regiments. The Guards appealed against this and Queen Victoria decided that the Queen's or First Colour should be crimson and the Regimental or Second Colour the Great Union. It was also decided at this time that the crimson Colonel's, Lieutenant-Colonel's and Major's Colour would now represent, respectively, the Queen's Colour of the 1st, 2nd and 3rd Battalions, and so it has remained.

GRENADIER GUARDS

At the Restoration this regiment was, in fact, two; one raised in England in 1660, the other made up of those who had been in exile with the King at Dunkirk. At this time the Royal Standard is described as being plain white with 'C.R.' and a crown painted in gold; all the other Colours were white with the red cross of St George covering the whole flag, each having a different company badge in the centre.

These two regiments amalgamated to form one in 1665 and at a Review in 1669, the Royal Standard had changed to crimson with the cypher and crown embroidered in gold. The three senior officers' colours were all white with the red cross, the Colonel's showing a crown, the Lieutenant-Colonel's a crown and 'C.R.' and the Major's as for the Lieutenant-Colonel's but with a crimson 'pile wavy' added. The 1st Captain's and remaining company colours were as already described.

The colours of this regiment are again recorded at the Coronation of James II and it is interesting to see them described as:

Royal Standards: Crimson, embroidered in the centre with the royal

28

29

30

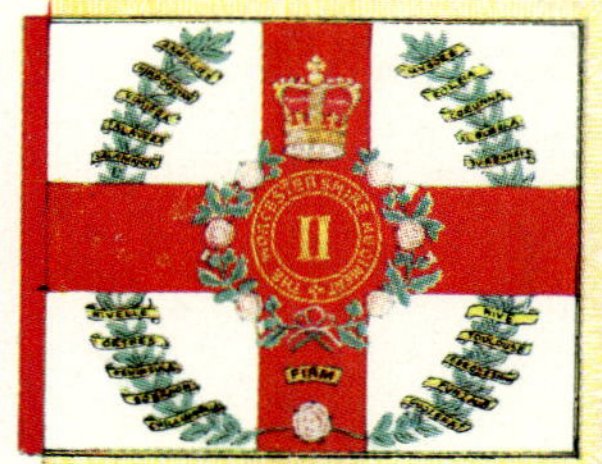

31

32

33

34

35

36

Plate 5

(28) Regimental Colour, 2nd Foot, 1st Bn The Queens (Royal West Surrey Regt). In use from 10th July 1847 until 10th July, 1947. (29 and 30) Queen's and Regimental Colours of 2nd Battalion, 24th Foot, presented in 1880. Later 2nd Bn The South Wales Borderers. (31) Regimental Colour, 2nd Battalion, Worcestershire Regiment. Presented by HRH The Prince of Wales, 12th June 1894. (32) Regimental Colour, 1st Battalion, The Royal Welsh Fusiliers. Presented by HM The Queen on the 23rd July 1954. (33) Queen's Colour, 1st Battalion, The Royal Scots. Presented by HRH The Princess Royal, 4th October, 1957. (34) Queen's Colour, The Duke of Edinburgh's Royal Regiment (Berkshire and Wiltshire). Presented by HRH The Duke of Edinburgh, 1959. (35) Regimental Colour, 1st Battalion, Durham Light Infantry, presented in 1955. (36) Regimental Colour, 2nd Battalion, The York and Lancaster Regiment, presented in 1927.

crown and 'J.R.' interlaced in gold.

Colonel's: Plain crimson, no design.

Lieutenant-Colonel's: White, with red cross throughout and the Imperial crown painted in gold.

Major's: As Lieutenant-Colonel's, with crimson 'pile wavy' issuing out of the top left hand corner.

1st Captain's Company: As Lieutenant-Colonel's, with King's Cypher and crown in the centre. The remaining nineteen companies were the same, except that each succeeding captain added another cypher and crown; the last and 20th company showed 20 of these.

The reign of James II was short as were the Colours of this design; by 1693 the company ensigns were again painted with their respective badges and the number, in Roman numerals, added in the upper canton.

From the end of the 17th Century until the middle of the 18th the only major change in design, was the addition of the white saltire and blue field of St Andrew to mark the Act of Union in 1707.

Minor changes were made, however, in the Royal Standard, which have been passed down to the present day, and to help reference, these and its later design are now covered together.

The official title of this flag is now 'The Queen's Company Colour, the Royal Standard of the Regiment'. It is normally carried by the 1st or Queen's Company and only on ceremonial occasions when the Sovereign is present. Tradition keeps it fringeless and of the old large size. It is also the personal gift of the Sovereign to the Grenadier Guards and a new one is usually presented at the beginning of each reign.

In 1706, a replacement standard—for one shot to pieces at the Battle of Hochstett—included, as well as the royal cypher of Queen Anne and crown, the quarterly arms of the four kingdoms. That is the rose—England, thistle—Scotland, fleur-de-lys—France, and the harp of Ireland. With the union of England and Scotland in 1707 this design was re-arranged to show the rose and thistle joined and placed in the first and fourth quarter, the fleur-de-lys in the second and the harp in the third. With the accession of George I in 1714, the arms of Hanover displaced the rose and thistle in the fourth quarter and the fleur-de-lys was removed in 1801. A small crown was added above each arm in 1743.

The final change, and the design seen today, came in 1837 and the accession of Queen Victoria when the arms of Hanover were removed. This standard, still crimson, now shows the royal cypher, reversed and interlaced with the Imperial Crown above. The quarterly arms, all crowned, are rose, first and third quarter, thistle in the second, and shamrock in the fourth.

In the period 1745-1768 the Union Colours of the Lieutenant-Colonel and Major were finally altered to crimson standards. Apart from the changes in size and the addition of battle honours and badges, the design was now established for the three senior officers' Colours which were to become the Queen's, or First Colours. These were:

Colonel's (1st Battalion): Crimson, Imperial crown in the centre.

Lieutenant-Colonel's (2nd Battalion): Crimson, small union in upper canton.

Major's (3rd Battalion): Crimson, as Lieutenant-Colonel's but with gold blaze or 'pile wavy' issuing from the union.

A stand of colours, 3rd Battalion Grenadier Guards, 1896. The central badge on the Regimental Colour is that of the 21st Company. The sentry in the picture—when the battalion was stationed at the Tower of London—is Private John Leary who enlisted in 1877. He wears the Soudan Medal and Khedive's Star for the 1884-85 Soudan Campaign. Note the long service stripes.

Plate 6

37

(37) The Colours of the 1st Battalion, The North Staffordshire Regiment. This was the last black regimental colour to be carried in the British Army.

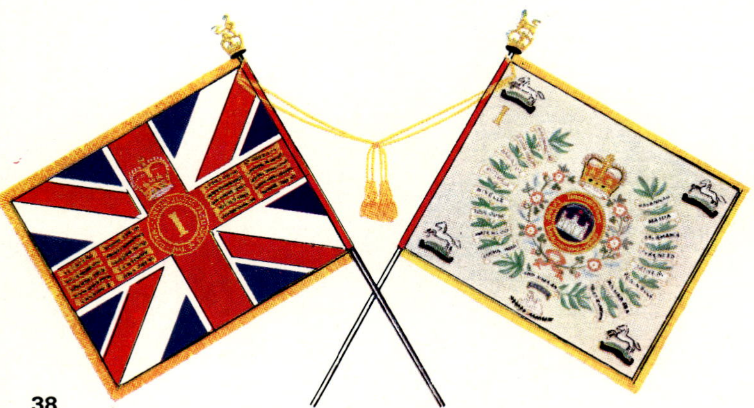

38

(38) The last Colours of The Royal Inniskilling Fusiliers before forming the new Regiment 1st Royal Irish Rangers.

39

(39) Colours of the Portsmouth Division, Royal Marines, presented by HRH The Duke of Edinburgh in 1956.

The addition of the red saltire of St Patrick in 1801 completed the Union flag and the basic design of Regimental Colour. Nowadays, as well as the central company badge, are added all battle honours scrolls and the number of the battalion in Roman numerals, in the upper canton. Incidentally, the central Company or Captain's badge, of which the Grenadiers have thirty, are borne in the Regimental Colours in strict rotation, irrespective of whether that company belongs to the particular battalion. If, for example, the 1st Captain's, or Queen's Company, badge is at present borne by the 1st Battalion and the 2nd Company Badge is shown on the 2nd Battalion's when these Colours are renewed they will be replaced by 3rd and 4th Company Badges.

Company badges are also made into Company Colours, 20in by 18in size, and mounted on a 7ft 7in pole. This Colour also gives the battalion and the abbreviation of the company, eg, 'R.F.' (Right Flank), 'B' (B Company). There is also a Company Colour for the Guards Parachute Company.

The small Company Colour of the Queen's Company is buried with the Sovereign, a custom started at the funeral of King Edward VII in 1910. The Grenadier Guards Company Badges are as follows:

1st or Queen's Company:	The Royal Crest in gold, a crowned lion standing on a large crown.
2nd:	A red Tudor rose with a white centre.
3rd:	A fleur-de-lys.
4th:	A portcullis with chains hanging from it.
5th:	A white rose in a glory or sun.
6th:	A thistle and rose, stalked and leaved.
7th:	The harp of Ireland.
8th:	The red dragon of Wales, on a green mount.
9th:	A white greyhound, with a red collar, standing on a green mount.
10th:	A sun in splendour with a human face.
11th:	A white unicorn of Scotland, gorged with a golden prince's coronet and chain, on a green mount.
12th:	A white antelope, gorged with a ducal crown and chain, standing on a green mount.
13th:	A white hart, gorged with a ducal crown and chain, on a green mount.
14th:	A white falcon with wings expanded, perched on the barrel of a close golden fetterlock.
15th:	A red rose with green stalks and leaves.
16th:	A white swan with expanded wings, gorged with a ducal crown and chain on a green mount.
17th:	A white falcon, corwned and bearing a sceptre, standing on the stump of a tree, out of which is growing a branch with three roses, one white and two red.
18th:	A trunk of a tree with three leaves sprouting.
19th:	A golden sceptre and sword proper.
20th:	A green oak tree on a green mount. In the branches of the tree may be seen the head of Charles II.
21st:	A sun rising behind clouds.
22nd:	A beacon or cresset with flames.
23rd:	Silver ostrich feathers, crossed.
24th:	A white hart with golden antlers springing from the gate of a golden triple towered castle.
25th:	A red cross of St George on a silver shield.
26th:	A golden lion rampart, crowned, standing near to eight billets on a blue shield.
27th:	The badge of the Order of the Bath, a device comprising the rose, thistle and shamrock.
28th:	Three crests of German origin, emanating from Saxony, Brunswick and Hanover.
29th:	A shamrock.
30th:	Out of a ducal Coronet appears a piller crowned with a coronet from which issues a plume of three peacocks feathers. The arms of Saxony are shown on the pillar.

NOTE: The first twenty of these badges were granted by Charles II in 1661; 21, 22, 23, and 24 by Queen Anne in 1713 and the remainder by Queen Victoria in 1855.

HM King George V (centre) with officers of the King's (or 1st) Company of the Grenadier Guards in April 1926. The company commander (a major) is seated left while the company second-in-command (a captain) is seated right with the CSM behind him. Note the King's Colour, the old large size, with cypher and Imperial Crown.

COLDSTREAM GUARDS

This regiment has the longest service on the English Establishment. Its history can, with certainty, be traced back to 1650. In February, 1661 it became a regiment of Foot Guards marching from Coldstream, on the River Tweed.

At the review in Hyde Park, in 1669, already mentioned under the previous section, a Colour of the Coldstream's is described as green with six white balls and a red cross. This is probably the ensign of the 6th Captain's company; as such, the balls would be arranged on the cross.

The facings of the regiment were changed to blue in 1685 although this colour was prominent on the regiment's standards as early as 1670. At the Coronation of James II in 1685, the Colours of this regiment, consisting of 12 companies were described as:

Colonel's: Plain blue, no design.

Lieutenant-Colonel's: Blue, with a white cross throughout surmounted by a crimson cross.

Major's: As Lieutenant-Colonel's, but with a white 'pile wavy' issuing out of the top left hand corner.

1st Captain's Company: As Lieutenant-Colonel's, but with the Roman numeral I painted in white in the upper canton. Each succeeding Captain had a different number so the last company showed IX.

The king directed that the 2nd Regiment of Foot Guards Colours were to agree more with those of the 1st Regiment and the blue field, already described, was changed to white. The Roman numbers on the Captain's Colour was now placed in the centre with the Imperial Crown above.

In 1696 William granted the Star of the Garter, the regiment's badge, and eleven company badges. The Colonel's Colour was crimson; the Lieutenant-Colonel's white with red St George's Cross, a Garter Star in the centre and crown above; the Major's the same with a pile wavy; Captain's white with St George's Cross, the 5th, 6th and 9th with Garter Star the other with Royal Badges.

Between 1707 and 1716 the Lieutenant-Colonel's and Major's Colours became crimson and by 1751 the regiments Colours are:

Colonel's: Crimson, star of the Garter in the centre, Imperial Crown above.

Lieutenant-Colonel's: Crimson, design as Colonel's but with the Union in the upper canton.

Major's: Same as Colonel's but with a Union in the upper canton, from the lower canton of which issues a gold 'pile wavy'.

Captain's: The Great Union, in the centre a Company badge with the crown above and the number of the Company in the upper or dexter canton.

Apart from the addition of the red saltire of St Patrick to complete the union in 1801, the design of the Colours changed very little. However, the Coldstream Guards also carry the 'Sphinx' as a battle honour badge on all their Colours.

The Coldstream Guards do not carry a Royal Standard but during the reign of William IV they were presented with two State Colours by the king. These are still used and carried by a Guard of Honour, mounted on State occasions at which the Sovereign is present.

Both these Colours are crimson of the old large size, fringed in gold and with crimson and gold cords and tassels. They are also similar in design, with the Star of the Order of the Garter within a Union Wreath, all worked in gold, in the centre and the Imperial Crown above. Both colours also have a silver Sphinx, between two golden branches of laurel, in each of the four corners. The earlier standard, however, has a single blue scroll with the word 'EGYPT' in gold placed under the central badge, whilst on the later one the scroll and 'EGYPT', in gold, appear above each of the Sphinx's. The first of these two State Colours also carries the battle honours 'LINCELLES', 'TALAVERA', 'BARROSA', 'PENINSULA', and 'WATERLOO'. The second shows these five plus 'INKERMAN', 'ALMA' and 'SEVASTOPOL' which were added about 1855.

As in the Grenadier Guards the Colonel's, Lieutenant-Colonel's and Major's Colours have become the Queen's Colours of the 1st, 2nd, and 3rd Battalions. These are now:

1st Battalion: Crimson, star of the Order of the Garter in the centre and Imperial Crown above. Immediately below the star a battle honour scroll inscribed 'SOUTH AFRICA 1899-1902', and below this the Sphinx superscribed 'EGYPT'. The remaining battle honours are arranged in vertical rows on either side of the central badges.

2nd Battalion: As 1st, but with a small union flag in the upper left hand corner, next to the pike.

3rd Battalion: As 2nd, with the addition of a gold pile wavy.

The Coldstream Guards have 24 Company badges, which as well as being borne, in rotation, on the Regimental Colours are also made up as Company Colours. The badges are:

1st Company:	A white lion on a green mount, surmounted by an imperial crown.
2nd:	The Prince of Wales's feathers in silver, with gold quills, encircled by the coronet of Edward the Black Prince.
3rd:	A white and black spotted panther, having flames of fire emitted from the mouth and ears, on a green mount.
4th:	Crossed swords, with points upwards, in silver. The hilt and pommel in gold.
5th:	The St George and Dragon.
6th:	A red rose with golden seeds and green thorns in a garter.
7th:	A centaur provided with a bow and arrow on a green mount.
8th:	Two crossed sceptres in gold.
9th:	The knot of the collar of the Order of the Garter.
10th:	A carbuncle in gold.
11th:	A white boar, passant, bistted and tusked in gold on a green mount.
12th:	A dun cow, on green mount.
13th:	A red and white rose impaled with a golden pomegrante bearing green leaves.
14th:	A white horse, galloping on a green mount.
15th:	The crown of Charlemange in gold.
16th:	The same badge as given for 28th Company Grenadier Guards.
17th:	The Royal cypher of Queen Victoria in gold.
18th:	A white tiger gorged with a ducal crown and chain on a green mount.
19th:	A red rose with golden seeds and green thorns in the collar of the Garter.
20th:	The red cross of St George within the Garter collar.
21st:	A black eagle with wings expanded with a Glory around the head.
22nd:	Two green laurel branches crossed issuing from a crown.
23rd:	The Crest of General Monck.
24th:	The Crest of the Duke of Cambridge.

These badges were granted as follows:

1st to 9th:	William III	—	1696
10th to 13th:	George I	—	1716
14th & 15th:	George II	—	1729
16th:	George IV	—	1814
Remainder:	Queen Victoria	—	1900

SCOTS GUARDS

Up until 1707 Scotland maintained its army under a separate establishment, 'His Majesty's Foot Guards' being one of these regiments, raised on May 1, 1661. In 1713, when it merged into the British Army, the regiment became The Third Regiment of Foot Guards, in 1831 it was changed to Scots Fusilier Guards and finally in 1877 to Scots Guards.

The first Colours granted to this regiment of Guards were given by Charles II in 1650. These are described as:

Colonel's: Blue, with the Royal Arms, without a crown, arranged quarterly. That is, Scotland—first and fourth, England and France—second quarter, and Ireland—third.

Lieutenant-Colonel's: Blue, with a white unicorn.

Major's: Blue, with lion rampant.

1st Captain's: Blue, with three fleur-de-lys.

2nd Captain's: Blue, a golden lion rampant on a blue shield.

3rd Captain's: Blue, three golden lions passant.

4th Captain's: Blue, a golden harp.

All these standards bore the design on one side only, on the other in

Adjutant and an ensign of the Coldstream Guards display the second of the two State Colours which is basically crimson and of the older large size.

large golden letters the words 'Covenant, For Religione, King and Kingdoms'.

Colours issued in 1662 were red with a saltire of a white St Andrew's Cross on a blue field with a crowned thistle in the centre and the motto 'NEMO ME IMPONE LACESSIT' surrounding this.

James II changed this design in 1685 and these were the last Scottish Colours of the regiment. They were:

Colonel's: Plain white, no design.

Lieutenant-Colonel's: White saltire of St Andrew on a blue field.

Major's: Same as Lieutenant-Colonel's with a red 'pile wavy' on the arm of the cross, issuing from the upper corner near the pike head.

1st Captain's: As the Lieutenant-Colonel's but with the numeral I in silver in the centre on the blue above the cross.

With the Act of Union in 1707, the colours added the St George's Cross over St Andrew's and so lost their typical Scottish design. By 1712, the senior officers were similar to the other two regiments of Guards, viz, Colonel's crimson; Lieutenant-Colonel's and Major's, the Union, but with their own distinctive central badges.

One small difference in the central design, adopted at this time and which may still be seen, is the feature of adding latin mottoes on scrolls

Colours of the 3rd Battalion Scots Guards in 1898 showing the Queen's Colour (Major's), on left decorated as described on the opposite page. Regimental Colour bearing the badge of the 17th Company is on right. Far left is the RSM, on right is the Drill Sergeant and in the centre two ensigns.

below all this regiment's badges. The other, which is less obvious, is that the company badges are very warlike in character and this is because Scottish kings did not adopt individual badges as the English kings did. These emblems are not, therefore, purely Scottish in character, but are contrived with this fighting regiment in mind.

The years 1712 to 1729 saw the adoption of the crimson standards for Colonel, Lieutenant-Colonel and Major and were similar in basic size and design as the 1st and 2nd regiments. This trend has continued right up to the present day, so most of the changes are described in the sections on Grenadier and Coldstream Guards. The Scots, however, follow the Coldstreams in adding to all their Colours the Sphinx and 'EGYPT' as a battle honour badge for the campaign in 1801.

The Scots Guards also possess a State Colour which was presented by Queen Victoria in 1899. This colour is carried only by Guards of Honour mounted on State occasions at which the Sovereign is present.

It is made of crimson silk, 6ft by 5ft and fringed. In the centre is the Star of the Order of the Thistle within its collar and encircled by a union wreath all embroidered in gold. Above this central design is the Imperial Crown and below the silver Sphinx and scroll 'EGYPT'. The following battle honours arranged on two circular branches of immortelles, all in gold, are: 'DETTINGEN', 'LINCELLES', 'TALAVERA', 'BARROSA', 'PENINSULA', 'WATERLOO', 'ALMA', 'INKERMAN', 'SEVASTOPOL', 'EGYPT 1882', 'TEL-EL-KEBIR', and 'SUAKIN 1885'.

The present Queen's Colours of Scots Guards bear the badges of the original Colonel, Lieutenant-Colonel and Major as laid down by Queen Anne in 1712, and are recorded as:

Colonel's (1st Battalion): Crimson, in the centre the red lion rampant of Scotland on a yellow shield, with the motto 'EN FERUS HOSTIS' (Behold a Fierce Enemy) below, and the Imperial Crown above.

Lieutenant-Colonel's (2nd Battalion): Crimson, in the centre a red and white rose and thistle issuing from one stem with the motto 'UNITA FORTIOR' (In Unity is Strength) below, and the crown above. In addition, a small Union flag in the dexter canton.

Major's (3rd Battalion): Crimson, and bears the badge of a Star of the Order of the Thistle with the motto 'SEMPER PARATUS' (Always Ready). This Colour also has the small Union flag in the dexter canton.

In addition, all these three standards show the typical Sphinx badge with the word 'EGYPT' and the general arrangement of four vertical rows of battle honour scrolls with one central, 'FRANCE AND FLANDERS, 1914-18', between motto and Sphinx.

The Regimental Colours are Union flags of usual Guards pattern already described, only the badges and mottoes distinguished them as belonging to the Scots Guards. The Company Colours are blue silk, and again as already described, each bears its allotted Company Badge, motto and number. In the dexter canton, embroidered in gold, '1st (or 2nd) Bn. S.G.' and in the sinister canton or opposite corner the abbreviation of the company, eg, 'R.F.' (Right Flank), or 'C' ('C' Company).

The Company Badges are as follows:

1st Company:	A red lion standing on an imperial crown all on a silver shield. Motto: 'IN DEFENSIO' ('In Defence').
2nd:	A hand grenade with a lighted fuse. Motto: 'TERROREM AFFAERO' ('I bring terror').
3rd:	The red rampant lion of Scotland. Motto: 'INTEPIDUS' ('Undaunted').
4th:	The cross with a representation of St Andrew, upon a star of silver, all under a thistle. Motto: 'NEMO ME IMPUNE LACESSIT' ('No one provokes me with impunity').
5th:	A red lion passant and full faced, on a gold shield. Motto: 'TIMERE NESCIUS' ('I do not know fear').
6th:	A blue griffin, on a gold shield. Motto: 'BELLOQUE FEROX' ('And ferocius in war').
7th:	A phoenix issuing from flames on a green mount. Motto: 'PER FUNERA VITAM' ('Thro' death to life').
8th:	A thunderbolt with silver wings. Motto: 'HORROR UBIQUE' ('Dread everywhere').
9th:	A cannon represented as though in the act of firing a shot. Motto: 'CONCUSSAE CADENT URBES' ('The cities crashing fall').
10th:	A salamander standing amidst flames. Motto: 'PASCUA NOTA MIHI' ('Pastures known to me').
11th:	A cross of St Andrew on a blue shield. Motto: 'IN HOC SIGNO VINCES' ('Under this banner you will conquer').
12th:	A group of war trophies. Motto: 'HONORE PRAEFERO' ('I put forth my honours').
13th:	A Talbot passant on a green mount, all in a gold shield. Motto: 'INTAMINATA FIDE' ('With faith unsullied').
14th:	A label of the Duke of Connaught, viz, a red cross on the centre point and blue fleur-de-lys on the other two. Motto: 'TE DUCE VINCIMUS' ('With you leading, we conquer').
15th:	A Galley of Lorne on a silver shield. Motto: 'NE OBLIVISCARIS' ('Lest you forget').
16th:	Half rose and thistle joined. Motto: 'FECIT EOS IN GENTEM UNAM' ('He made them into one people').
17th:	The crest of HRH Prince Albert. Motto: 'TREU UND FEST' ('True and fast').
18th:	The crest of 3rd Earl of Linlithgow. Motto: 'SI POSSIM' ('If I can').
19th:	A silver unicorn rampant on a blue shield. Motto: 'RES NON VERBA' ('Deeds not words').
20th:	A red lion rampant on a gold shield. Motto: 'FORWARD.'
21st:	The badge of the Order of the Thistle. Motto: 'FORTIS IN ARDUIS' ('Steadfast thro' difficulties').
22nd:	The Union Flag on a shield. Motto: 'NIL DESPERANDUM' ('Nothing is hopeless').
23rd:	A thistle encircled by the collar of the Order of the Thistle. Motto: 'NOLI ME TANGERE' ('Do not touch me').
24th:	A red fleur-de-lys on a gold shield. Motto: 'PRO PATRIA' ('For our country').

NOTE: The first thirteen badges were granted in 1712 by Queen Anne: 14, 15 and 16 in 1887 and 17 in 1900 by Queen Victoria and the remainder by King Edward VII in 1901.

THE IRISH GUARDS

The history of the original regiment goes back to 1642, it having been raised just before the battle of Edgehill. It was practically destroyed later at the Battle of Naseby. Charles II formed another regiment in 1662 which subsequently entered the service of France, merged with the 92nd Regiment of the French Army at the time of the revolution, but then disbanded.

The present Irish Guards were raised in 1900 by Queen Victoria to commemorate the bravery of those Irish Line regiments which had fought in South Africa.

Very little is known about the Colours of the earlier regiment, except that they were of yellow taffeta with crimson and gold cords. They also followed the pattern of the 1st Foot Guards at the time of the Restoration, in having 'severall Badges proper for that Kingdome' (Ireland), although no description of these has survived.

The Irish Guards have no Royal Standard or State Colour. The present Queen's Colour is crimson, with the Royal Cypher in the centre surrounded by the collar of the Order of St Patrick, all in gold, and surmounted by the Imperial Crown. Battle honour scrolls follow the usual arrangement.

The Great Union is the Regimental Colour, with its appropriate Company Badge in the centre, Imperial Crown above, Company number below, and again, the usual arrangement of battle honours.

The following is a list of Company badges granted in 1901:

1st Company:	The Royal Cyphers of Queen Victoria and Edward VII in gold.
2nd:	The Cypher of HRH The Duke of Connaught, in gold, surrounded by a green wreath of shamrocks.
3rd:	A gold harp within a blue circle on which is the motto of the Order of St Patrick.
4th:	The badge of the Order of St Patrick.
5th:	Two crossed swords, gold pommels and hilts, surmounted by a shamrock.
6th:	The knot and two roses from the collar of the Order of St Patrick.
7th:	The red cross of St Patrick on a silver shield.
8th:	The crest of Field Marshall Earl Roberts.
9th:	The crest of Ireland within the collar of the Order of St Patrick.
10th:	A silver, six pointed star and the red hand of Ulster.
11th:	A sea horse gorged with a rural crown of Belfast.
12th:	A castle in flames—from the arms of Dublin.
13th:	A gold ancient Crown of Ireland—from the arms of Munster.
14th:	An Irish Wolfhound statant.
15th:	A half black eagle joined by an upward raised arm grasping a sword.
16th:	A pierced silver narcissus.

WELSH GUARDS

This regiment was not raised until February, 1915, and formed the guard at Buckingham Palace on St David's Day of that year, just a week after its formation.

The Welsh Guards have no Royal Standard or State Colour and, like the Irish Guards, carry their Queen's Colour when State Colours are ordered to be borne. The Queen's Colour is crimson with a golden Dragon passant in the centre, a scroll underneath with the motto 'CYMRU AM BYTH' (Wales for Ever') and the crown above. The battle honour scrolls are arranged in two vertical rows on either side of the central badge. The Regimental Colour is the Great Union and bears the fourteen Company badges in rotation.

The Company Colours are quite distinctive being more like cavalry

The presentation of colours to the 1st Bn The Royal Inniskilling Fusiliers by HRH The Duke of Gloucester, Colonel-in-Chief of the Regiment, at Templar Barracks, Kahawa, Kenya, 20th February 1962.

HRH The Prince Philip, Duke of Edinburgh, presenting new colours to the Queen's Royal Surrey Regiment (now 1st Bn The Queen's Regiment), 1960.

guidons than the square flags of the other Guards' regiments.

These are described as:

1st, or Prince of Wales Company:	Red, three silver lions passant.
2nd:	Green, golden eagles with wings spread.
3rd:	Quarter panels in gold and crimson, each with a lion passant, of opposite hue.
4th:	Crimson, with a lion rampant in gold.
5th:	Gold, with a lion rampant in crimson.
6th:	Eight vertical stripes of alternating silver and red with a black lion rampant.
7th:	Quarter panels in silver and gold, three black boars' heads in first and fourth and a lion rampant in second and third.
8th:	Red, with three silver chevrons.
9th:	Red, a chevron between three gold lioncels rampant.
10th:	Black, a chevron between three silver fleurs-de-lys.
11th:	Green, a chevron between three silver wolves' heads.
12th:	Silver, a chevron between three black ravens.
13th:	Black, with a silver lion rampant.
14th:	Silver, three black boars' heads.
15th:	Silver, a black cross and between each limb a black bird.

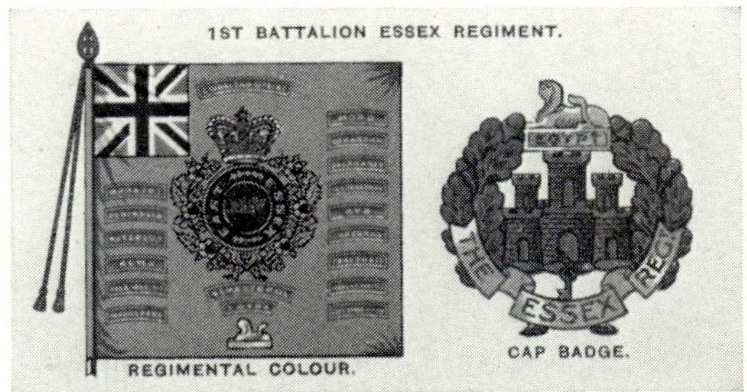

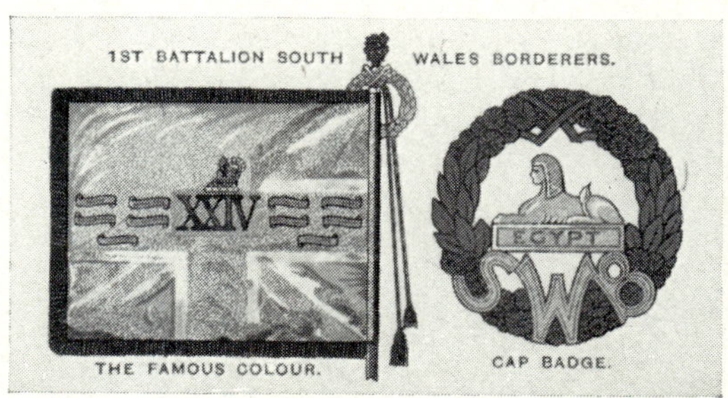

Among the scores of cigarette card sets available prior to the 1939-1945 war were some exquisitely printed issues devoted to regimental standards and colours. For the modern student of the subject they make invaluable references and are well worth seeking out. The two examples shown are from a set titled 'Regimental Standards and Cap Badges' issued by John Player & Sons (Imperial Tobacco Co) in the late 1920s. Top is the 1st Bn, Essex Regt, which retained the 1844 pattern large size colour with spearhead on pike (cf. picture on page 12). Below it is portrayed the tattered and faded 1st Bn South Wales Borderers' Queen's Colour which was heroically retrieved by two subalterns after the defeat by the Zulus at Isandhlwana in 1879. It carries the wreath of immortelles subsequently presented by Queen Victoria.

Appendix 1:

A list of those Regiments granted special badges in the Royal Clothing Warrant 1747

NOTES

(1) The badge is always placed in the centre of both the King's and Regimental Colour; the number of the regiment on both colours shown in the upper canton.

(2) The corner badges do not appear on the King's Colour.

(3) The description given refers to the 2nd or regimental colour.

(4) Titles given in parentheses are post 1881 titles.

1st or Royal Regiment (Royal Scots)

Blue, with 'GR' in gold on a blue field within the green circle of St Andrew. In the three corners a crown and thistle; scroll without motto.

2nd or Queens Own Royal Regiment (Royal West Surrey Regiment)

Sea green, with 'CARA' in gold on red within the garter (garter blue), in the three corners the white lamb; scroll with motto 'PRISTINAE VIRTUTIS MEMOR.'

NB: The letters 'CR' stand for Carolina Regina and the two A's the terminal letters of the previous words.

3rd or the Buffs (East Kent Regiment)

Buff, with a green dragon above the scroll with 'VETERI FRONDESCET HONORE'. In the three corners a crown and rose (crimson).

NB: No crown above badge.

4th or Kings Own Royal Regiment (Royal Lancaster Regiment)

Blue, 'GR' in gold on a red field within the garter and plain white scroll below. In the three corners the crowned lion of England in gold.

NB: No scroll on King's colour.

5th Regiment (The Northumberland Fusiliers)

Pale yellow, St George in white armour on a brown horse, and green dragon. In the three corners a crown and rose.

NB: No crown above badge.

6th Regiment (The Royal Warwickshire Regiment)

Deep yellow, in the centre a white antelope on a green mount; plain scroll. In the three corners a crown and rose.

NB: No crown above badge.

7th or the Royal English Fusiliers (The Royal Fusiliers)

Blue, a red rose in a red field within the garter; plain scroll. In the three corners the white horse on a green mount.

The Regimental Colours of the 1st Battalion, The Royal Highland Fusiliers, being paraded at the unique honour of the Freedom of Iserlohn, Germany. In the centre is the Honorary Third Colour of the Regiment, described on pages 20 and 22.

The York and Lancaster Regiment march past City Hall on its way to lay-up its Colours in Sheffield Cathedral for the last time. The Regiment served its country for 210 years and its 22 battalions won 59 battle honours alone during the First World War.

8th or The King's Regiment (Liverpool Regiment)

Blue, the white horse on a red field within the garter; scroll with motto 'NEG ASPERA TERRENT'. In the three corners 'GR' and crown in gold.

18th The Royal Irish (The Royal Irish Regiment)

Blue, a gold harp; motto 'VIRTUTIS NAMURCENSIS PRAEMIUM'. In the three corners the golden lion of Nassau in a blue field, surrounded by golden billets.

21st or Royal North British Fusiliers (The Royal Scots Fusiliers)

Blue, the thistle on a blue ground within the green circle of St Andrew. In the three corners 'GR' and crown in gold. Plain scroll.

23rd or The Royal Welch Fusiliers (The Royal Welch Fusiliers)

Blue, three white feathers issuing for a golden Prince's coronet. Scroll with motto 'ICH DIEN'. In the upper corner a gold sun rising behind a green hill, blue sky. A red dragon on blue field, lower left hand corner and the three feathers and coronet on a red field in the lower right hand corner.

NB: No crown above badge and no label on the King's colour.

27th or The Inniskilling Regiment (The Royal Inniskilling Fusiliers)

Buff, the castle of Inniskilling white in a blue field and 'INNISKILLING' in gold; plain scroll.

NB: No crown above badge.

Appendix 2: Sizes of Colours

PERIOD AND AUTHORITY	SIZE OF COLOURS		SIZE OF PIKE
	Width	Depth on Pike	
1747 Regulations	6ft 6in	6ft 2in	
1768 Clothing Warrant	6ft 6in	6ft 0in	9ft 10in including spear and ferrule
1855 Clothing Warrant	6ft 0in	5ft 6in	9ft 10in including spear and ferrule
1858 Clothing Warrant	4ft 0in	3ft 6in	9ft 10in including Royal Crest
1868 Queen's Regulations	3ft 9in	3ft 0in	9ft 10in including Royal Crest
	(Exclusive of fringe)		
1873 Queen's Regulations	3ft 9in	3ft 0in	8ft 7in including Royal Crest
	(Exclusive of fringe)		
1898 Clothing Regulations	3ft 9in	3ft 0in	8ft 7½in including Royal Crest
	(Exclusive of fringe)		

The New Colour Guard at the amalgamation parade of the Queen's Royal Surrey Regiment, formerly the Queen's Royal Regiment and the The East Surrey Regiment, at Bury St. Edmunds, 22nd April 1960

Note: *The pictures on pages 43, 44, 47, 48, 50, and 56, are by courtesy of* Soldier *Magazine.*

Appendix 3:

LIST OF LINE INFANTRY REGIMENTS—NUMBERS, TITLES & FACINGS.

THE FOLLOWING SYMBOLS, SHOWN IN REMARKS COLUMN, REFERS TO THOSE REGIMENTS. WHO UNDER THE CARDWELL REFORMS OF 1881, WERE AUTHORIZED TO CARRY WHITE REGIMENTAL COLOURS, IE. RED ST GEORGES CROSS ON A WHITE FIELD. BUT AT SOMETIME LATER CHANGED THEIR FACING COLOUR

* * – WHITE REGIMENTAL COLOUR NEVER ISSUED TO 1ST BATTALION.
* Ꝗ – WHITE REGIMENTAL COLOUR NEVER ISSUED TO 2ND BATTALION.
* † – WHITE REGIMENTAL COLOUR CARRIED BY 1ST BATTALION DURING YEARS SHOWN IN BRACKETS.
* ‡ – WHITE REGIMENTAL COLOUR CARRIED BY 2ND BATTALION DURING YEARS SHOWN IN BRACKETS.

REGT No	SECONDARY TITLE AS AT 1815	PRE-1881 FACING COLOUR	1881 REORGANIZATION		FACING COLOUR CHANGE	LATER TITLE	AMALGAMATION DISBANDMENT ETC	REMARKS
			TITLE	FACING COLOUR				
1ST	THE ROYAL SCOTS	BLUE	THE ROYAL SCOTS (THE ROYAL REGT)	BLUE	–	THE ROYAL SCOTS (THE LOTHIAN REGT)		
2ND.	THE QUEENS ROYAL REGIMENT	SEA GREEN - 1748 BLUE	THE QUEENS (ROYAL WEST SURREY REGT)	BLUE	–	THE QUEENS ROYAL REGT (WEST SURREY)	2, 31 & 70 1ST BN THE QUEENS REGIMENT - 1966	1ST BN CARRIED A STAND OF COLOURS FOR EXACTLY 100 YEARS (10/7/1847 – 10/7/1947)
3RD	EAST KENT OR THE BUFFS	BUFF	THE BUFFS (EAST KENT REGIMENT)	WHITE	BUFF - 1890	THE BUFFS (ROYAL EAST KENT REGT)	3, 50 & 97 2ND BN THE QUEENS REGIMENT - 1966	* ‡ (1886 - 1891)
4TH.	THE KINGS OWN	BLUE	THE KINGS OWN (ROYAL LANCASTER REGIMENT)	BLUE	–	THE KINGS OWN ROYAL REGT (LANCASTER)	4, 34 & 55 THE KINGS OWN ROYAL BORDER REGT 1959	
5TH	THE NORTHUMBERLAND REGIMENT OF FOOT	GOSLING GREEN	THE NORTHUMBERLAND FUSILIERS	WHITE	GOSLING GREEN - 1899	THE ROYAL NORTHUMBERLAND FUSILIERS	1BN ROYAL REGT OF FUSILIERS 1968	* Ꝗ PARADES SMALL GREEN "DRUMMERS COLOUR" ON ST GEORGES DAY
6TH	1ST WARWICKSHIRE REGIMENT	YELLOW	THE ROYAL WARWICKSHIRE REGIMENT	BLUE		THE ROYAL WARWICKSHIRE FUSILIERS - 1963	2BN ROYAL REGT OF FUSILIERS - 1968	
7TH	THE ROYAL FUZILEERS	BLUE	THE ROYAL FUSILIERS (CITY OF LONDON REGT)	BLUE		THE ROYAL FUSILIERS (CITY OF LONDON REGT)	3BN ROYAL REGT OF FUSILIERS - 1968	
8TH	THE KINGS REGT	BLUE	THE KINGS (LIVERPOOL REGIMENT)	BLUE		THE KINGS REGIMENT (LIVERPOOL)	8, 63 & 96 THE KINGS REGIMENT (MANCHESTER & LIVERPOOL) 1958	
9TH	THE EAST NORFOLK REGIMENT	YELLOW	THE NORFOLK REGT	WHITE	YELLOW - 1905 'ROYAL' - 1935	THE ROYAL NORFOLK REGIMENT	9 & 12 1ST ROYAL ANGLIAN REGIMENT - 1959	† (1887 - 1909) ‡ (1892 - 1919) ROYAL IN 1935 BUT AUTHORIZED YELLOW FACINGS
10TH.	THE NORTH LINCOLNSHIRE REGIMENT	YELLOW	THE LINCOLNSHIRE REGIMENT	WHITE	ROYAL BLUE 1946 BLUE - 1949	THE ROYAL LINCOLNSHIRE REGIMENT	10, 48 & 58 2ND ROYAL ANGLIAN REGIMENT 1960	* Ꝗ 1ST BN CARRIED COLOURS (YELLOW) 1864 - 1960 2ND BN CARRIED COLOURS (YELLOW) 1859 - 1960.
11TH	THE NORTH DEVONSHIRE REGIMENT	LINCOLN GREEN	THE DEVONSHIRE REGT	WHITE	LINCOLN GREEN - 1905	THE DEVONSHIRE REGT.	11, 39 & 54 THE DEVONSHIRE AND DORSET REGT 1958	* Ꝗ
12TH	THE EAST SUFFOLK REGIMENT	YELLOW	THE SUFFOLK REGT.	WHITE	YELLOW 1899	THE SUFFOLK REGT.	9 & 12 1ST ROYAL ANGLIAN REGIMENT 1959	* Ꝗ 1ST BN CARRIED A STAND OF COLOURS (YELLOW) 1849 TO 1955
13TH	1ST SOMERSETSHIRE REGIMENT	YELLOW BLUE - 1843	PRINCE ALBERTS LIGHT INFANTRY (SOMERSETSHIRE REGT)	BLUE		THE SOMERSET LIGHT INFANTRY (PRINCE ALBERTS)	13, 32 & 46 1ST BN THE LIGHT INFANTRY 1966	
14TH	THE BUCKINGHAMSHIRE REGIMENT	BUFF	THE PRINCE OF WALES OWN (WEST YORKSHIRE REGIMENT.)	WHITE	BUFF - 1900	THE WEST YORKSHIRE REGT (PRINCE OF WALESS OWN)	14 & 15 THE PRINCE OF WALESS OWN REGIMENT OF YORKSHIRE - 1958	* Ꝗ
15TH	THE YORKSHIRE (EAST RIDING) REGT	YELLOW	THE EAST YORKSHIRE REGT (THE DUKE OF YORKS OWN)	WHITE		THE EAST YORKSHIRE REGT (THE DUKE OF YORKS OWN)	14 & 15 AS ABOVE.	
16TH	THE BEDFORDSHIRE REGIMENT	YELLOW	THE BEDFORDSHIRE REGIMENT	WHITE		THE BEDFORDSHIRE & HERTFORDSHIRE REGIMENT	16, 44 & 56 3RD. ROYAL ANGLIAN REGIMENT - 1958	
17TH	THE LEICESTERSHIRE REGIMENT	WHITE	THE LEICESTERSHIRE REGIMENT	WHITE	'ROYAL' - 1946 PEARL GREY 1931	THE ROYAL LEICESTERSHIRE REGIMENT	4TH ROYAL ANGLIAN REGIMENT - 1964 DISBANDED - 1970	
18TH	THE ROYAL IRISH REGT	BLUE	THE ROYAL IRISH REGT	BLUE		THE ROYAL IRISH REGT	DISBANDED - 1922	
19TH	THE 1ST YORKSHIRE (WEST RIDING) REGT	GRASS GREEN	THE PRINCESS OF WALES'S OWN (YORKSHIRE REGT.)	WHITE	GRASS GREEN - 1899	THE GREEN HOWARDS (ALEXANDRA, PRINCESS OF WALESS OWN YORKSHIRE REGT.		* Ꝗ

REGT^L Nº	SECONDARY TITLE AS AT 1815	PRE 1881 FACING COLOUR	1881 REORGANIZATION		FACING COLOUR CHANGE	LATER TITLE	AMALGAMATION, DISBANDMENT, ETC	REMARKS
			TITLE	FACING COLOUR				
20TH	THE EAST DEVONSHIRE REGIMENT	YELLOW	THE LANCASHIRE FUSILIERS	WHITE		THE LANCASHIRE FUSILIERS	4 TH BN ROYAL REGT OF FUSILIERS DISBANDED - 1968	1ST BN CARRIED A STAND OF PRE 1881 (YELLOW) COLOURS FROM 1670 UNTIL 1934
21 ST	ROYAL SCOTCH FUZILEERS - 1748 THE ROYAL NORTH BRITISH FUZILEERS	BLUE	THE ROYAL SCOTS FUSILIERS	BLUE		THE ROYAL SCOTS FUSILIERS	21, 71 & 74 THE ROYAL HIGHLAND FUSILIERS - 1958	
22 ND	THE CHESHIRE REGT	BUFF	THE CHESHIRE REGT	WHITE	BUFF - 1904	THE CHESHIRE REGT*		* ‡ (1889 - 1919)
23 RD	THE ROYAL WELSH FUZILEERS	BLUE	THE ROYAL WELSH FUSILIERS	BLUE		THE ROYAL WELCH FUSILIERS		2ND BN CARRIED A SET OF COLOURS FROM 1859 - 1954
24 TH	THE WARWICKSHIRE REGIMENT	GRASS GREEN	THE SOUTH WALES BORDERERS	WHITE	GRASS GREEN - 1905	THE SOUTH WALES BORDERERS	24, 41 & 69 ROYAL REGIMENT OF WALES - 1968	* & BOTH BATT'S BEAR SILVER WREATHS OF IMMORTALS ON THE STAFF OF THE QUEENS COLOUR, TO COMMEMORATE QUEEN VICTORIAS WREATH ON THE COLOUR RECOVERED AFTER ISANDHLWANA - 1879 NOW BORNE AS ROYAL REGT WALES
25 TH	THE KING'S OWN BORDERERS REGT	BLUE	THE KINGS OWN SCOTTISH BORDERERS	BLUE		THE KINGS OWN SCOTTISH BORDERERS		
26 TH	THE CAMERONIAN REGIMENT	YELLOW	1/THE CAMERONIANS (SCOTTISH RIFLES) (108 TH - 2 BN)	CONVERTED TO RIFLE REGIMENT CEASED TO CARRY COLOURS		THE CAMERONIANS (SCOTTISH RIFLES)	DISBANDED - 1968	
27 TH	THE INNISKILLING REGIMENT	BUFF	1/THE ROYAL INNISKILLING FUSILIERS (108 TH. - 2 BN)	BLUE	SPECIAL AUTHORITY TO RETAIN BUFF REGT^L COLOURS - 1939	THE ROYAL INNISKILLING FUSILIERS	27, 83, 86, 87, 89 & 108 1 ST BN THE ROYAL IRISH RANGERS 1968	BLUE REGT^L COLOUR NEVER ISSUED TO 1ST BN. PAIR CARRIED 1869 TO 1939 (BUFF)
28 TH	THE NORTH GLOUCESTER - SHIRE REGIMENT	YELLOW	1/THE GLOUCESTERSHIRE REGIMENT (61 ST. - 2 BN)	WHITE	PRIMROSE YELLOW - 1929	THE GLOUCESTERSHIRE REGIMENT		* YELLOW FROM 1868 - 1952 PRIMROSE YELLOW FROM 1952
29 TH	THE WORCESTERSHIRE REGIMENT	YELLOW	1/THE WORCESTERSHIRE REGIMENT (36 TH. - 2 BN)	WHITE	GRASS GREEN - 1920	THE WORCESTERSHIRE REGIMENT	29, 36, 45 & 95 THE WORCESTERSHIRE AND SHERWOOD FORESTERS REGIMENT - 1970	† (1913 - 1960)
30 TH	THE CAMBRIDGESHIRE REGIMENT	PALE YELLOW	1/THE EAST LANCASHIRE REGIMENT. (59 TH - 2 BN)	WHITE		THE EAST LANCASHIRE REGIMENT	30, 40, 47, 59, 81 & 82 THE QUEENS LANCASHIRE REGIMENT - 1970	WHITE COLOUR SINCE 1950
31 ST	THE HUNTINGDONSHIRE REGIMENT	BUFF	1/THE EAST SURREY REGIMENT. (70 TH - 2 BN)	WHITE.		THE EAST SURREY REGT	2, 31 & 70 1 ST BN THE QUEENS REGIMENT - 1966	WHITE COLOUR SINCE 1903
32 ND	THE CORNWALL REGT	WHITE	1/THE DUKE OF CORNWALLS LIGHT INFANTRY (46 TH - 2 BN)	WHITE		THE DUKE OF CORNWALL'S LIGHT INFANTRY	13, 32 & 46 1ST BN THE LIGHT INFANTRY - 1966	
33 RD	THE 1 ST YORKSHIRE (WEST RIDING) REGT.	SCARLET	1/THE DUKE OF WELLINGTON'S REGT (WEST RIDING) (76 TH - 2 BN)	WHITE	SCARLET - 1905	THE DUKE OF WELLINGTONS REGT. (WEST RIDING)		SCARLET FACINGS ARE THE SAME AS WHITE FOR REGT^L COLOUR - I.E. RED ST GEORGES CROSS ON WHITE FIELD. REGT ALSO CARRIES A PAIR OF HONORARY COLOURS
34 TH	THE CUMBERLAND REGIMENT	YELLOW	1/THE BORDER REGT (55 TH - 2 BN)	WHITE	YELLOW - 1913	THE BORDER REGIMENT	4, 34 & 55 THE KING'S OWN ROYAL BORDER REGT. - 1959	*
35 TH	THE SUSSEX REGIMENT	ORANGE BLUE 1832	1/THE ROYAL SUSSEX REGIMENT (107 TH - 2 BN)	BLUE		THE ROYAL SUSSEX REGT.	3RD. BN. THE QUEEN'S REGIMENT	'ROYAL' SINCE 1832
36 TH	THE HEREFORDSHIRE REGIMENT	GOSLING GREEN	2/THE WORCESTERSHIRE REGIMENT (29 TH - 1 BN.)	WHITE	GRASS GREEN - 1920	THE WORCESTERSHIRE REGIMENT	29, 36, 45 & 95 THE WORCESTERSHIRE & SHERWOOD FORESTERS REGIMENT - 1970	‡ (1894 - 1930)
37 TH.	THE NORTH HAMPSHIRE	YELLOW	1/THE HAMPSHIRE REGT (67 TH. - 2 BN)	WHITE	YELLOW - 1904	THE ROYAL HAMPSHIRE REGIMENT		* 'ROYAL' IN 1946
38 TH	THE 1 ST STAFFORDSHIRE REGIMENT	YELLOW	1/THE SOUTH STAFFORD - SHIRE REGIMENT (80 TH - 2 BN)	WHITE	YELLOW - 1936	THE SOUTH STAFFORDSHIRE REGIMENT	38, 64, 80 & 98 THE STAFFORDSHIRE REGIMENT - 1958	
39 TH	THE DORSETSHIRE REGT	PEA GREEN	1/THE DORSETSHIRE REGIMENT (54 TH. - 2 BN)	WHITE	GRASS GREEN - 1904	THE DORSET REGIMENT	11, 39 & 54 THE DEVONSHIRE AND DORSET REGT - 1958	† (1890 1912)
40 TH	THE 2ND SOMERSETSHIRE REGIMENT	BUFF	1/THE PRINCE OF WALES'S VOLUNTEERS (SOUTH LANCASHIRE REGT (82 ND - 2 BN)	WHITE	BUFF - 1933	THE SOUTH LANCASHIRE REGT (PRINCE OF WALES'S VOLUNTEERS)	30, 40, 47, 59, 81 & 82 THE QUEEN'S LANCASHIRE REGIMENT - 1970	† (1927 - 1955)

REGTL Nº	SECONDARY TITLE AS AT 1815	PRE 1881 FACING COLOUR	1881 REORGANIZATION		FACING COLOUR CHANGE	LATER TITLE	AMALGAMATION DISBANDMENT ETC	REMARKS
			TITLE	FACING COLOUR				
41ST		SCARLET WHITE	1. THE WELSH REGT. (69 TH - 2 BN)	WHITE		THE WELCH REGIMENT	24, 41 & 69 ROYAL REGIMENT OF WALES - 1968	
42ND	THE ROYAL HIGHLAND REGIMENT	BLUE	1/ THE BLACK WATCH (ROYAL HIGHLANDERS) (73 RD - 2 BN)	BLUE		THE BLACK WATCH (THE ROYAL HIGHLAND REGIMENT.)		
43RD	THE MONMOUTHSHIRE REGT. (LIGHT INFANTRY)	WHITE	1/ THE OXFORDSHIRE LIGHT INFANTRY (52 ND - 2 BN)	WHITE		THE OXFORDSHIRE AND BUCKINGHAMSHIRE LIGHT INFANTRY	1 ST. BN. THE ROYAL GREEN JACKETS - 1966	
44TH	THE EAST ESSEX REGT	YELLOW	1/ THE ESSEX REGIMENT (56 TH - 2 BN.)	WHITE	PURPLE - 1936	THE ESSEX REGIMENT	16, 44 & 56 3RD BN. THE ROYAL ANGLIAN REGT 1958	1ST BN. CARRIED COLOURS PRESENTED IN 1857 UNTIL AMALGAMATION IN 1958
45TH	THE NOTTINGHAMSHIRE REGIMENT	DARK GREEN	1/ THE SHERWOOD FORESTERS (DERBYSHIRE REGIMENT) (95 TH - 2 BN)	WHITE	LINCOLN GREEN - 1913	THE SHERWOOD FORESTERS (NOTTINGHAMSHIRE AND DERBYSHIRE REGIMENT)	29, 36, 45 & 95 THE WORCESTERSHIRE AND SHERWOOD FORESTERS REGIMENT - 1970	† (1912 - 1935)
46TH	THE SOUTH DEVONSHIRE REGIMENT	PALE YELLOW	2/ THE DUKE OF CORNWALL'S LIGHT INFANTRY (32 ND - 1 BN)	WHITE		THE DUKE OF CORNWALL'S LIGHT INFANTRY	13, 32 & 46 1 ST. BN. THE LIGHT INFANTRY - 1966	
47TH	THE LANCASHIRE REGIMENT	WHITE	1/ THE LOYAL NORTH LANCASHIRE REGIMENT (81 ST - 2 BN)	WHITE		THE LOYAL REGIMENT (NORTH LANCASHIRE)	30, 40, 47, 59, 81 & 82 THE QUEENS LANCASHIRE REGIMENT - 1970	
48TH	THE NORTHAMPTONSHIRE REGIMENT	BUFF	1/ THE NORTHAMPTONSHIRE REGIMENT (58 TH - 2 BN)	WHITE	BUFF - 1927	THE NORTHAMPTONSHIRE REGIMENT	10, 48 & 58 2ND BN THE ROYAL ANGLIAN REGT. - 1960	1 ST. BN. RETAINED ITS WHITE COLOUR, PRESENTED IN 1889, UNTIL AMALGAMATION IN 1960
49TH	THE HERTFORDSHIRE REGIMENT	GREEN	1/ PRINCESS CHARLOTTE OF WALES'S (BERKSHIRE REGIMENT.) (66 TH - 2 BN.)	WHITE	TI BLUE - 1885	THE ROYAL BERKSHIRE REGIMENT	49, 62, 66 & 99 THE DUKE OF EDINBURGH'S ROYAL REGIMENT - 1959	* 'ROYAL' IN 1885 A SET OF COLOURS (WHITE REGT'L) WAS MADE BUT NEVER ISSUED. THEY WERE GIVEN TO THE REGT IN 1920.
50TH	THE WEST KENT REGT	BLACK	1/ THE QUEEN'S OWN ROYAL WEST KENT REGT. (97 TH. - 2 BN)	BLUE		THE QUEEN'S OWN ROYAL WEST KENT REGT.	3, 50 & 97 2 ND. BN. THE QUEEN'S REGIMENT - 1966	
51ST	THE 2ND. YORKSHIRE (WEST RIDING) REGT (LIGHT INFANTRY)	GRASS GREEN BLUE - 1821	1/ THE KINGS OWN LIGHT INFANTRY (SOUTH YORKSHIRE REGIMENT) (105 TH - 2 BN.)	BLUE		THE KINGS OWN YORKSHIRE LIGHT INFANTRY	2 ND. BN. THE LIGHT INFANTRY - 1966	
52ND.	THE OXFORDSHIRE REGT (LIGHT INFANTRY)	BUFF	2/ THE OXFORDSHIRE LIGHT INFANTRY (43 RD - 1 BN.)	WHITE		THE OXFORDSHIRE AND BUCKINGHAMSHIRE LIGHT INFANTRY	1 ST. BN. ROYAL GREEN JACKETS - 1966	ɸ 2 ND. BN. - COLOURS USED SINCE 1868
53RD	THE SHROPSHIRE REGT.	SCARLET	1/ THE KING'S SHROPSHIRE LIGHT INFANTRY (85 TH - 2 BN.)	BLUE		THE KING'S SHROPSHIRE LIGHT INFANTRY	3 RD. BN. THE LIGHT INFANTRY - 1968	1 ST BN. - RED ST. GEORGE'S CROSS ON WHITE FIELD FROM 1877 UNTIL 1954
54TH	THE WEST NORFOLK REGIMENT	GREEN	2/ THE DORSETSHIRE REGT (39 TH - 1 BN)	WHITE	GRASS GREEN - 1904	THE DORSET REGIMENT	11, 39 & 54 THE DEVONSHIRE AND DORSET REGT. - 1958	‡ (1887 - 1909)
55TH.	THE WESTMORELAND REGIMENT	GREEN	2/ THE BORDER REGT (34 TH - 1 BN)	WHITE	YELLOW - 1913	THE BORDER REGIMENT	4, 34 & 55 THE KINGS OWN ROYAL BORDER REGT - 1959	‡ (1888 - 1924)
56TH	THE WEST ESSEX REGIMENT	PURPLE	2/ THE ESSEX REGT. (44 TH - 1 BN.)	WHITE	PURPLE - 1936	THE ESSEX REGIMENT	16, 44 & 56 3RD BN. THE ROYAL ANGLIAN REGT. - 1958	ɸ 2 ND BN. CARRIED COLOURS PRESENTED IN 1864. NO OTHERS WERE ISSUED.
57TH	THE WEST MIDDLESEX REGIMENT	YELLOW	1/ THE MIDDLESEX REGT (DUKE OF CAMBRIDGE'S OWN) (77 TH. - 2 BN)	WHITE	LEMON YELLOW - 1902	THE MIDDLESEX REGT (DUKE OF CAMBRIDGE'S OWN)	4 TH. BN. THE QUEEN'S REGIMENT - 1966.	
58TH	THE RUTLANDSHIRE REGIMENT	BLACK	2/ THE NORTHAMPTONSHIRE REGIMENT (48 TH - 1 BN.)	WHITE	BUFF - 1927	THE NORTHAMPTONSHIRE REGIMENT	10, 48 & 58 2 ND. BN. THE ROYAL ANGLIAN REGT. - 1960	2 ND BN - KEPT 6FT × 5FT 6IN COLOURS (BLACK REGT'L) FROM 1860 UNTIL 1960. THESE WERE THE LAST BRITISH INFANTRY COLOURS CARRIED IN ACTION - LAING'S NEK, SOUTH AFRICA 1881
59TH	THE 2ND NOTTINGHAMSHIRE REGIMENT	WHITE	2/ THE EAST LANCASHIRE REGIMENT (30 TH - 1 BN)	WHITE		THE EAST LANCASHIRE REGIMENT	30, 40, 47, 59, 81 & 82 THE QUEEN'S LANCASHIRE REGIMENT - 1970	
60TH	THE ROYAL AMERICAN REGIMENT	BLUE REGT'L COLOUR	THE KINGS ROYAL RIFLE CORPS	CONVERTED TO RIFLE REGT CEASED TO CARRY COLOURS		THE KING'S ROYAL RIFLE CORPS.	2 ND. BN. ROYAL GREEN JACKETS - 1966	
61ST	THE SOUTH GLOUCESTERSHIRE REGIMENT	BUFF	2/ THE GLOUCESTERSHIRE REGIMENT (28 TH - 1 BN)	WHITE	PRIMROSE YELLOW 1929	THE GLOUCESTERSHIRE REGIMENT		ɸ

Appendix 3:

REGT[L] Nº	SECONDARY TITLE AS AT 1815	PRE 1881 FACING COLOUR	1881 REORGANIZATION TITLE	1881 REORGANIZATION FACING COLOUR	FACING COLOUR CHANGE	LATER TITLE	AMALGAMATION DISBANDMENT ETC	REMARKS
62ND	THE WILTSHIRE REGT.	BUFF	1/ THE WILTSHIRE REGT. (DUKE OF EDINBURGH'S) (99 TH. - 2 BN.)	WHITE	BUFF - 1905	THE WILTSHIRE REGT. (DUKE OF EDINBURGH'S)	49, 62, 66 & 99 THE DUKE OF EDINBURGH'S ROYAL REGIMENT - 1959	*
63RD	THE WEST SUFFOLK REGIMENT	DEEP GREEN	1/ THE MANCHESTER REGT. (96 TH - 2 BN)	WHITE	DEEP GREEN - 1937	THE MANCHESTER REGT	8, 63 & 96 THE KING'S REGIMENT (MANCHESTER & LIVERPOOL) - 1958	*
64TH	THE 2ND STAFFORDSHIRE REGIMENT	BLACK	1/ THE NORTH STAFFORD-SHIRE REGIMENT (98 TH - 2 BN)	WHITE	BLACK 1937	THE NORTH STAFFORDSHIRE REGIMENT	38, 64, 80 & 98 THE STAFFORDSHIRE REGIMENT - 1958	*
65TH	THE 2ND YORKSHIRE (NORTH RIDING) REGT.	WHITE	1/ THE YORK & LANCASTER REGIMENT (84 TH - 2 BN)	WHITE		THE YORK & LANCASTER REGIMENT	DISBANDED - 1968	
66TH	THE BERKSHIRE REGT	GOSLING GREEN	2/ PRINCESS CHARLOTTE OF WALES'S (BERKSHIRE REGIMENT) (49 TH - 1 BN)	WHITE	BLUE - 1885	THE ROYAL BERKSHIRE REGIMENT	49, 62, 66 & 99 THE DUKE OF EDINBURGH'S ROYAL REGIMENT - 1959	‡ (FROM 1882) 'ROYAL' - 1885
67TH	THE SOUTH HAMPSHIRE REGIMENT	YELLOW	2/ THE HAMPSHIRE REGT (37 TH - 1 BN)	WHITE	YELLOW - 1904	THE ROYAL HAMPSHIRE REGIMENT		‡ (FROM 1889 'ROYAL' - 1946
68TH	THE DURHAM REGT. (LIGHT INFANTRY)	BOTTLE GREEN	1/ THE DURHAM LIGHT INFANTRY (106 TH - 2 BN)	WHITE	DARK GREEN - 1903	THE DURHAM LIGHT INFANTRY	4 TH BN THE LIGHT INFANTRY - 1968 DISBANDED - 1968	† (1888 - 1911)
69TH	THE SOUTH LINCOLN-SHIRE REGIMENT	GREEN	2/ THE WELCH REGT. (41 ST. - 1 BN)	WHITE		THE WELCH REGIMENT	24, 41 & 69 THE ROYAL REGIMENT OF WALES - 1968	‡ (FROM 1899)
70TH	THE GLASGOW LOWLAND REGIMENT	BLACK	2/ THE EAST SURREY REGIMENT (31 ST. - 1 BN)	WHITE		THE EAST SURREY REGT	2, 31 & 70 1 ST. BN THE QUEEN'S REGIMENT - 1966	2 ND BN CARRIED A PAIR OF COLOURS (BLACK REGT[L]) FOR 78 YEARS - 1867 TO 1945
71ST	HIGHLAND REGIMENT (LIGHT INFANTRY)	BUFF	1/ THE HIGHLAND LIGHT INFANTRY (CITY OF GLASGOW REGIMENT) (74 TH - 2 BN.)	YELLOW	BUFF - 1899	THE HIGHLAND LIGHT INFANTRY (CITY OF GLASGOW REGIMENT)	21, 71 & 74 THE ROYAL HIGHLAND FUSILIERS - 1958	1 ST. BN. NEVER ISSUED WITH YELLOW REGT[L] COLOUR
72ND	HIGHLAND REGIMENT	YELLOW	1/ THE SEAFORTH HIGH-LANDERS (ROSS SHIRE BUFFS, THE DUKE OF ALBANY'S) (78 TH - 2 BN)	YELLOW	BUFF - 1899	THE SEAFORTH HIGHLANDERS (ROSS SHIRE BUFFS, THE DUKE OF ALBANY'S)	72, 78 & 79 THE QUEEN'S OWN HIGHLANDERS - 1960	
73RD	HIGHLAND REGIMENT	DARK GREEN	2/ THE BLACK WATCH (ROYAL HIGHLANDERS) (42 ND - 1 BN)	BLUE		THE BLACK WATCH (THE ROYAL HIGHLAND REGT)		2 ND. BN. - BLUE FROM 1887
74TH	HIGHLAND REGIMENT	WHITE	2/ THE HIGHLAND LIGHT INFANTRY (CITY OF GLASGOW REGIMENT) (71 ST - 1 BN)	YELLOW	BUFF 1899	THE HIGHLAND LIGHT INFANTRY (CITY OF GLASGOW REGIMENT)	21, 71 & 74 THE ROYAL HIGHLAND FUSILIERS - 1958	2 ND BN NEVER ISSUED WITH YELLOW REGT[L] COLOUR. ALSO HAS WHITE HONORARY COLOUR FOR BATTLE OF ASSAYE
75TH	HIGHLAND REGIMENT	YELLOW	1/ THE GORDON HIGHLANDERS (92 ND - 2 BN)	YELLOW		THE GORDON HIGHLANDERS		
76TH		SCARLET	2/ THE DUKE OF WELLINGTON'S REGT. (WEST RIDING) (33 RD - 1 BN)	WHITE	SCARLET - 1905	THE DUKE OF WELLINGTON'S REGT. (WEST RIDING)		
77TH	THE EAST MIDDLESEX REGIMENT	YELLOW	2/ THE MIDDLESEX REGT (DUKE OF CAMBRIDGE'S OWN) (57 TH - 1 BN)	WHITE	LEMON YELLOW 1902	THE MIDDLESEX REGT (DUKE OF CAMBRIDGE'S OWN)	4 TH BN. THE QUEEN'S REGIMENT - 1966	φ
78TH	HIGHLAND REGIMENT (OR THE ROSS SHIRE BUFFS)	BUFF	2/ THE SEAFORTH HIGHLANDERS (ROSS SHIRE BUFFS, THE DUKE OF ALBANY'S) (72 ND - 1 BN)	YELLOW	BUFF - 1899	THE SEAFORTH HIGHLANDERS (ROSS-SHIRE BUFFS, THE DUKE OF ALBANY'S)	72, 78 & 79 THE QUEEN'S OWN HIGHLANDERS - 1960	
79TH	REGIMENT OF CAMERON HIGHLANDERS	DARK GREEN BLUE - 1873	THE QUEEN'S OWN CAMERON HIGHLANDERS	BLUE		THE QUEEN'S OWN CAMERON HIGHLANDERS	72, 78 & 79 AS ABOVE	
80TH	STAFFORDSHIRE VOLUNTEERS	YELLOW	2/ THE SOUTH STAFFORD-SHIRE REGIMENT (38 TH - 1 BN)	WHITE	YELLOW - 1936	THE SOUTH STAFFORDSHIRE REGIMENT	38, 64, 80 & 98. THE STAFFORDSHIRE REGIMENT - 1958	‡ (FROM 1906)
81ST		BUFF	2/ THE LOYAL NORTH LANCASHIRE REGIMENT (47 TH - 1 BN)	WHITE		THE LOYAL REGIMENT (NORTH LANCASHIRE)	30, 40, 47, 59, 81 & 82 THE QUEEN'S LANCASHIRE REGIMENT 1970	
82ND	PRINCE OF WALES'S VOLUNTEERS	YELLOW	2/ THE PRINCE OF WALES'S VOLUNTEERS (SOUTH LANCASHIRE REGIMENT) (40 TH - 1 BN)	WHITE	BUFF - 1933	THE SOUTH LANCASHIRE REGIMENT (PRINCE OF WALES'S VOLUNTEERS)	30, 40, 47, 59, 81 & 82 AS ABOVE	‡ (FROM 1911)

REGT[L] Nº	SECONDARY TITLE AS AT 1815	PRE 1881 FACING COLOUR	1881 REORGANIZATION		FACING COLOUR CHANGE	LATER TITLE	AMALGAMATION DISBANDMENT ETC	REMARKS
			TITLE	FACING COLOUR				
83RD		YELLOW	1/THE ROYAL IRISH RIFLES (86 TH - 2 BN.)	CONVERTED TO RIFLE REGT CEASED TO CARRY COLOURS		THE ROYAL ULSTER RIFLES	27. 83, 86, 87, 89 & 108 THE ROYAL IRISH RANGERS - 1968	
84TH	YORK & LANCASTER REGIMENT	YELLOW	2/THE YORK & LANCASTER REGIMENT (65 TH - 1BN.)	WHITE		THE YORK & LANCASTER REGIMENT	DISBANDED - 1968	‡ (FROM 1891)
85TH	BUCKS VOLUNTEERS (LIGHT INFANTRY)	YELLOW	2/THE KINGS SHROPSHIRE LIGHT INFANTRY (53 RD - 1BN.)	BLUE		THE KINGS SHROPSHIRE LIGHT INFANTRY	3 RD. BN. THE LIGHT INFANTRY - 1968	2 ND BN - BLUE FROM 1935.
86TH	THE ROYAL COUNTY DOWN REGIMENT	BLUE	2/THE ROYAL IRISH RIFLES (83 RD - 1BN)	CONVERTED TO RIFLE REGT. CEASED TO CARRY COLOURS		THE ROYAL ULSTER RIFLES	27, 83, 86, 87, 89 & 108 THE ROYAL IRISH RANGERS - 1968	
87TH	THE PRINCE OF WALES'S OWN IRISH REGIMENT	GREEN	1/THE ROYAL IRISH FUSILIERS (PRINCESS VICTORIAS) (89 TH - 2BN)	BLUE		THE ROYAL IRISH FUSILIERS (PRINCESS VICTORIA'S)	27, 83, 86, 87, 89 & 108 AS ABOVE	
88TH	THE CONNAUGHT RANGERS	YELLOW	1/THE CONNAUGHT RANGERS (94 TH - 2BN)	GREEN		THE CONNAUGHT RANGERS	DISBANDED - 1922	1ST BN CARRIED A YELLOW COLOUR ISSUED IN 1877 UNTIL 1911.
89TH		BLACK	2/THE ROYAL IRISH FUSILIERS (PRINCESS VICTORIAS) (87 TH 1BN)	BLUE		THE ROYAL IRISH FUSILIERS (PRINCESS VICTORIA'S)	27, 83, 86, 87, 89 & 108 THE ROYAL IRISH RANGERS - 1968	UP TO 1889 - RED CROSS ST. GEORGE ON BLACK FIELD FROM 1889 - BLUE
90TH	THE PERTHSHIRE VOLUNTEERS	BUFF	2/THE CAMERONIANS (SCOTTISH RIFLES) (26 TH - 1BN)	CONVERTED TO RIFLE REGT CEASED TO CARRY COLOURS		THE CAMERONIANS (SCOTTISH RIFLES)	DISBANDED - 1968	
91ST	ARGYLLSHIRE REGT	YELLOW	1/PRINCESS LOUISE'S ARGYLL & SUTHERLAND HIGHLANDERS (93 RD - 2 BN)	YELLOW		THE ARGYLL & SUTHERLAND HIGHLANDERS (PRINCESS LOUISE)		
92ND	GORDON HIGHLANDERS	YELLOW	2/THE GORDON HIGHLANDERS (75 TH - 1BN)	YELLOW		THE GORDON HIGHLANDERS		
93RD	SUTHERLAND HIGHLANDERS	YELLOW	2/PRINCESS LOUISE'S ARGYLL & SUTHERLAND HIGHLANDERS (91 ST - 1BN.)	YELLOW		THE ARGYLL & SUTHERLAND HIGHLANDERS (PRINCESS LOUISE)		
94TH		GREEN	2/THE CONNAUGHT RANGERS (88 TH - 1BN)	GREEN		THE CONNAUGHT RANGERS	DISBANDED - 1922	
95TH		BLACK	2/THE SHERWOOD FORESTERS (DERBYSHIRE REGIMENT) (45 TH - 1BN)	WHITE	LINCOLN GREEN - 1913	THE SHERWOOD FORESTERS (NOTTINGHAMSHIRE AND DERBYSHIRE REGIMENT)	29, 36, 45 & 95 THE WORCESTERSHIRE & SHERWOOD FORESTERS REGIMENT - 1970	‡ (1891 - 1927)
96TH		YELLOW	2/THE MANCHESTER REGT (63RD - 1BN)	WHITE	DEEP GREEN - 1937	THE MANCHESTER REGT	8, 63 & 96 THE KINGS REGIMENT (MANCHESTER & LIVERPOOL) 1958	
97TH	THE QUEENS OWN REGIMENT	SKY BLUE	2/THE QUEEN'S OWN (ROYAL WEST KENT) (50 TH - 1BN)	BLUE		THE QUEEN'S OWN (ROYAL WEST KENT REGT)	3, 50 & 97 2ND BN. THE QUEENS REGIMENT - 1966	
98TH		WHITE	2/THE NORTH STAFFORDSHIRE REGIMENT (64 TH - 1 BN)	WHITE	BLACK - 1937	THE NORTH STAFFORDSHIRE REGIMENT	38, 64, 80 & 98 THE STAFFORDSHIRE REGIMENT - 1958	‡ (FROM 1876)
99TH	THE PRINCE OF WALES'S TIPPERARY REGIMENT	PALE YELLOW	2/THE WILTSHIRE REGT (DUKE OF EDINBURGHS)	WHITE	BUFF - 1905	THE WILTSHIRE REGT. (DUKE OF EDINBURGHS)	49, 62, 66 & 99 THE DUKE OF EDINBURGHS ROYAL REGIMENT 1959	ф
100TH	H.R.H. THE PRINCE REGENTS COUNTY OF DUBLIN REGT.	BLUE	1/THE PRINCE OF WALES'S LEINSTER REGIMENT (ROYAL CANADIANS) (109 TH - 2BN)	BLUE		THE PRINCE OF WALES'S LEINSTER REGIMENT (ROYAL CANADIANS)	DISBANDED - 1922	
101ST	THE DUKE OF YORK'S IRISH REGIMENT	WHITE	1/THE ROYAL MUNSTER FUSILIERS (104 TH - 2BN)	BLUE		THE ROYAL MUNSTER FUSILIERS	DISBANDED - 1922	
102ND	ROYAL MADRAS FUSILIERS - 1860	YELLOW	1/THE ROYAL DUBLIN FUSILIERS (103 RD 2BN)	BLUE		THE ROYAL DUBLIN FUSILIERS	DISBANDED - 1922	
103RD	ROYAL BOMBAY FUSILIERS	WHITE	2/THE ROYAL DUBLIN FUSILIERS (102 ND - 1BN)	BLUE		THE ROYAL DUBLIN FUSILIERS	DISBANDED - 1922	
104TH	BENGAL FUSILIERS - 1839	BUFF	2/THE ROYAL MUNSTER FUSILIERS (101 ST - 1BN)	BLUE		THE ROYAL MUNSTER FUSILIERS	DISBANDED - 1922	

REGT[L] NO	SECONDARY TITLE AS AT 1815	PRE 1881 FACING COLOUR	1881 REORGANIZATION		FACING COLOUR CHANGE	LATER TITLE	AMALGAMATION DISBANDMENT ETC	REMARKS
			TITLE	FACING COLOUR				
105TH	MADRAS LIGHT INFANTRY - 1839	PALE BUFF	2/ THE KING'S OWN LIGHT INFANTRY (SOUTH YORKSHIRE REGIMENT) (51 ST - 1 BN)	BLUE		THE KING'S OWN YORKSHIRE LIGHT INFANTRY	2ND BN THE LIGHT INFANTRY - 1966	
106TH	BOMBAY LIGHT INFANTRY - 1860	WHITE	2/ THE DURHAM LIGHT INFANTRY (68 TH - 1 BN)	WHITE		THE DURHAM LIGHT INFANTRY	4 TH BN THE LIGHT INFANTRY - 1968 DISBANDED - 1968	
107TH	BENGAL INFANTRY - 1854		2/ THE ROYAL SUSSEX REGIMENT (35 TH - 1 BN.)	BLUE		THE ROYAL SUSSEX REGIMENT	3RD BN THE QUEENS REGIMENT - 1966	
108TH	MADRAS INFANTRY REGIMENT - 1862	PALE YELLOW	2/ THE ROYAL INNISKILLING FUSILIERS (27TH - 1 BN)	BLUE		THE ROYAL INNISKILLING FUSILIERS	27 83, 86, 87, 89 & 108 1ST BN THE ROYAL IRISH RANGERS	2ND BN BLUE 1888 & 1906 DISBANDED 1922 REFORMED 1937 BUFF SINCE 1939
109TH	BOMBAY INFANTRY REGIMENT - 1853	WHITE	2/ THE PRINCE OF WALES'S LEINSTER REGIMENT (ROYAL CANADIANS) (100 TH - 1 BN)	BLUE		THE PRINCE OF WALES'S LEINSTER REGIMENT (ROYAL CANADIANS)	DISBANDED - 1922	
	95 TH (RIFLES) REGT OF FOOT	BLACK/UNIFORM GREEN	THE RIFLE BRIGADE (THE PRINCE CONSORTS OWN)	RIFLE BRIGADE HAS NEVER HAD COLOURS		THE RIFLE BRIGADE	3 RD BN ROYAL GREEN JACKETS 1966	
						THE PARACHUTE REGT FACINGS MAROON COLOURS AUTHORISED 1948		COLOURS FIRST PRESENTED TO THE THREE REGULAR BTNS IN 1950 BY GEORGE VI

TOP: The beginning—The Duke of Wellington's Regt, with new Honorary Colours, presented in Hong Kong, April 1969. ABOVE: The end—The Regimental Colours of the Durham Light Infantry laid-up in Durham Cathedral marking the disbandment of the Regiment in 1968.